The Lakeland Outpouring:

The Inside Story!

The Lakeland Outpouring:

The Inside Story!

By
Stephen R. Strader

With
Mary Achor

Foreword by Dr. Karl D. Strader

The Lakeland Outpouring: The Inside Story!

Published by:
Legacy Media Group
P.O. Box 870
Windermere, FL 34786 USA
www.LMGpublishing.com

Publishing for Generations

ISBN: 978-0-9820458-2-4

Printed in the United States of America by Epic Print Solutions

Dedication

I want to dedicate this book to all of those who have prayed so many hours for an outpouring of the Holy Spirit! Don't stop!

I want to thank my wife, Janice, for taking much of the burden of administration for our local church so that I could devote myself to the Outpouring, as well as all the journaling and writing for this book.

And I want to also thank C. Peter Wagner and the other apostles who risked their reputations to come and protect this Outpouring with their apostolic authority and to help me personally.

And much thanks goes to my dear friend, Mary Achor, an extraordinary historian and writer, who patiently pulled this all together for me.

"This is a stunning account of one of the great sovereign moves of God in the past 100 years. Stephen Strader's heart to steward what God has given us has enabled him to stay true to the outpouring of the Spirit in the midst of controversy and suspicion. I am thankful for this man of God and for this book as it will help all of us to plow through fields wrought with thorns and find the great treasure that was given to us in the Lakeland Outpouring."

--Bill Johnson
Bethel Church, Redding, CA
Author of *When Heaven Invades Earth* and *Face to Face with God*

"As I read Strader's book, I realized that ultimately, this outpouring will be remembered as a revelation of God's glory drenching both the humble and the hardhearted; and His grace kissing away the Judas and Thomas attitudes within us all.

This valuable book gives us an insider's glimpse into the glory of God revealed during the Lakeland Outpouring, the joys and challenges of hosting a revival, and the lessons learned. Strader's insights prepare us to contain the fullness of Christ and help us understand how to steward the measure we are receiving. Position yourself to receive more of God's loving presence and power. After all, He is not done with us yet!"

-- Julia Loren
Author of *Shifting Shadows of Supernatural Power*

"No one has been used of God more and taken less credit than Stephen Strader. There is a reason these great outpourings happen in his church."

--Doug Wead
Presidential historian and New York Times best-selling author.
He has been a religious advisor to two presidents and served in the White House of George H. W. Bush.

Every move of God carries both the divine and the natural element and ultimately must be measured by the fruit it produces. So it is with the Lakeland Outpouring! I have had the privilege to witness first-hand, both at home and around the world, the wonderful fruit of this remarkable move of God. Here is the story behind the story as Pastor Stephen Strader chronicles the epic journey of a people touched by God. The soaring highs of Gods glory and the devastating lows of human frailty are all part of this amazing pilgrimage. This book a must read for any person hungry for the move of God.

--Ron Johnson
Lead Apostle, Foundations International

"You will experience the transformation that empowered thousands as you read Strader's behind the scenes narrative of one of the most impacting outpourings of God's presence in modern history."

--Dr. Joshua Fowler
Legacy Life Church, Orlando, Florida
Author of *Access Granted* and *ID Required*

This is a remarkably candid account of one of the most remarkable moves of God in recent times. For all of the multitudes who were touched by this outpouring around the world, it left many questions which need answers. Many of those answers are in this book.

--Rick Joyner
MorningStar Ministries, Fort Mill, SC
Author of *The Final Quest* and *The Harvest*

Table of Contents

Foreword
By
Dr. Karl D. Strader

I couldn't be any more thankful that my son, Stephen, has put together this book that explains with pure accuracy the events and the reflections of the recent "Lakeland Outpouring."

With no hesitancy, I have endorsed this move of God as one of the greatest I've ever witnessed in my whole life. Even with one of the leaders and his "feet of clay," God overrode whatever damage that was done, by blessing untold thousands of people from around the world. It was no revival, that's for sure, but it was a special outpouring from heaven that went around the world through modern means of technology.

My son took the brunt of the criticism that came to us locally, but he has kept his integrity, and stayed on top of a very turbulent time. He has stayed sweet in his spirit and kept things going when it was almost impossible. God helped him, that's for sure.

I saw with my own eyes the thousands that gave their hearts to God, the other thousands that reported they were healed, the hours upon hours of the most intense worship at any large gathering I've ever witnessed, with special emphasis on young people, street people, addicts and you name it, glorifying and praising God. I saw absolutely nothing that was sponsored from the platform that was demonic. Jesus was lifted up from day one. The Bible was preached with fervor. The Holy Ghost was evident throughout the entire audience. The music was horrible for those of us that were older, but the new generation loved it!

With my Methodist background, my ultra-fundamentalist training, my 50 years with the Pentecostals and my 25 years with the Charismatics, I couldn't have been any more pleased. The insatiable hunger, the heavy-duty desperation for more of God was unbelievable.

From day one, being filled with the Holy Ghost at 25, I have loved the supernatural. But I know, as you should know, the fruit of the Spirit is just as supernatural as the Gifts of the Spirit; however, we don't have to choose which one, we can have both. Our church in Lakeland (I pastored the one church for 40 years) has always had an open door to the great moves of God in our time, and that's why I have a valid suspicion that that was one of the reasons God showed up here in particular. It surprised us all, like Peter standing at the door after we had prayed, but I give God all the glory!

Chapter One
Fresh Fire!

At the time this book was nearly completed, the Lakeland Outpouring was at Day 100. So much happened in the days following, it was difficult to keep up.

When we finally sent the book to the publisher, we had closed the Outpouring after 188 days, and Todd Bentley had resigned from Fresh Fire Ministries and was in counseling and restoration. It appears now that his earlier restoration process was either not complete or that the additional pressures of the Outpouring revealed deeper problems. Now, we are all praying deeply and compassionately for his complete healing and restoration.

We were also faced with the option to reject the work that the Holy Spirit accomplished during the Outpouring or to embrace it with joy. Like so many of the outpourings, revivals, and awakenings of the past, you can focus on the good or the bad. We have chosen to rejoice with those who received an impartation of the Holy Spirit. We have chosen to celebrate the miracles and the dynamic experiences of those who were positively impacted. We have chosen to reflect on the ways God led us through this experience so we can learn from our mistakes and capitalize on our successes.

And the self-cleaning, rushing river of God continues to bless and heal people in this next, most remarkable season at the Ignited Church.

Let me tell you about it.

Fresh Fire!

It was like a scene from *Field of Dreams.*

But instead of cars winding through Iowa cornfields, here they were rolling over flat, sandy Florida soil, past trees dripping with Spanish moss.

They were not heading for some mythical baseball game.

These cars were streaming down Florida back roads to the massive modern tents of the Lakeland Outpouring. They were coming to what they may have thought as a revival, but that was a misnomer. A revival is reviving something; we weren't reviving anything. This was an _outpouring_—a release of something fresh. It was the difference between a water bucket and the ocean, between a shower and Niagara Falls.

The people were coming, many for healing, yes—but all came seeking a powerful, profound, passionate outpouring of the Presence of God. And here they were finding it—in ways appropriate and meaningful for each.

People were coming from different religious traditions and backgrounds. They were at different maturity levels—spiritually, emotionally and physically. Folks came for different reasons—some to get healed or to get help. Others were observing out of curiosity. Spiritual leaders journeyed here, looking for greater impartation to help them in their ministry. Some were drawn because they themselves were in a dry place and were looking for fresh water. Hungry, thirsty, passionate.

People came to the services with different gift mixes. My wife, for example, is more administrative gifting; I am more apostolic gifting. So when we came to the meetings we had different desires and passions of what we wanted to receive to amplify our gifts. There were people coming to a meeting who were very sensitive to the Holy Spirit and responded accordingly. Others were resistant to the Spirit, so it took them a long time to warm up. Some rushed in, convinced that this was God, and they were coming to *get some.* Others tiptoed in, a little apprehensive, not really sure whether this was of God.

In any given service of 5,000 people there would be 5,000 different experiences. You personally might have been experiencing the fire of God, while the person next to you was experiencing the love of God. Another might be receiving the healing of God. Someone else might be having their emotions touched. That was one of the exciting, dynamic things about these meetings. So many had countless, desperate experiences, all in the Presence of God.

On the other side of the coin, the vast majority of the people also appeared to be experiencing a unity, a harmony, much like an orchestra. The Holy Spirit was the conductor, and sometimes there was a flute playing, sometimes a French horn; sometimes there were cymbal crashes. It flowed. All these individuals were intermingling and experiencing a sound, like an orchestra. That was the dynamics of the services.

I loved that. Here was the dynamic of worshipers in a unique experience of God, while that same group of people flowed together as an orchestra. All at the same time! One had only to look at the faces as they worshipped— upraised, glowing. It was a humbling thing.

Even walking through the tent prior to the services was humbling. People came early, and knelt, deep in prayer. Others lay prone on the ground, their arms outstretched in a cross, oblivious to the bustle about them, as new arrivals stepped carefully around and over them to find their own places. The atmosphere of the place had such a sweet spirit. Faces smiled at you—fellow conspirators in Jesus, anticipating the gifts of the evening.

And then it got loud.

For some, admittedly, it was too much. But for others—the young people or perhaps those wearing Harley-Davidson t-shirts—the music resonated for them in a way that no worship service had before. And it drew them in to worship Jesus Christ. And the glory fell—not just for them, but for all.

And Roy Fields sang:

**We are the generation
Who will stand and fight
In the midst of all the darkness
We'll carry the light.**

Every day of the Outpouring, we received the most astoundingly beautiful messages from people who had experienced the blessings of God in the

Outpouring. I want to share a handful with you. They speak so eloquently, it touches my heart and my tear ducts.

"Momma Julia's Rough Guide to Glory #2"

I went into the central, land-filled swamps of Florida over the weekend to see a reed swayed by the wind.

I went to see the tattooed and pierced holy man, Todd Bentley, a raving young man, moving counter culturally to the religious, well-dressed churchgoers of the day. Born centuries after John the Baptist, this Canadian evangelist epitomizes one whom Jesus called the least in the kingdom of heaven who is greater than John the Baptist. He is one reported to release the glory of God through the manifestation of healing in his meetings.

I went to see the crowds; to be able to say, "I was there" in case it becomes recorded as a historic event on the timeline of revival history.

I went to see what Jesus had to say about the ravings of the lunatic John the Baptist; to see what Matthew 11 is all about and undeniably saw that the kingdom of God has been forcefully advancing since the times of John the Baptist. The crowds who heard the music of the hour and rejoiced in the miracles mixed with those who did not dance or rejoice in the miracles of healing taking place all around them.

I had heard the reports about this 32-year-old Todd—some good, some bad. Like John the Baptist, the wild man, this young evangelist faced accusers who claimed, "He has a demon." He was quite the teenage sinner and openly admits a prison record. Like John the Baptist, Todd was in prison. He is also like Jesus in that he attracts the gluttons and drunkards, and is a friend of tax collectors, drug addicts, ex-cons, prostitutes and perverts, and all variety of "sinners." Jesus moved in the spirit, amazed the crowds by what He did and offended the minds of others by what He said.

I went out to see the reed swaying in the wind of the Holy Spirit - having heard about the instability of the reed and the strength of the wind.

Todd's past was dealt with early on before he was launched into ministry…and even later on. After being in international ministry for some years, Todd faced an emotional meltdown on a platform in England that was likely brought on by the haunting wounds of his youth that forced their way to the surface. His inner core being unable to withstand the pressures of constantly moving under the anointing of God and the scrutiny of men, begged for healing. At the urging of his board and fathers in the faith, Todd stepped aside for a full year to move deeply and willingly into the healing presence of Jesus. He embraced the ministry of many counselors to deal with root issues in his life—before they could manifest in sinful reactions.

I went out to see the reed swaying in the wind of the Holy Spirit and his skin.

Thank God, our skin is no longer under the condemning old covenant of Biblical, religious law. I had read the internet accounts from those offended by the music of the hour – the worship and the joy – whose orphan spirit caused them to shy away from the glory of God to scream out old covenant accusations against a brother, like, "Todd has tattoos that may mean satanic things and writing on skin is expressly forbidden in the Bible." I had peeked at his skin and saw the markings of a bond slave of Jesus Christ and the New Covenant covering the scars that slashed deeply into his wrists and arms and soul during his tumultuous Baal-worshipping youth. I saw the kanji lettering that gives honor to the *Great King*, and calls for equilibrium to be found in the middle of Him. I saw the Lion of Judah, the scriptures and scenes spread out haphazardly all over his body as if graffiti artists spray painted the outer walls of the temple. But it is this graffiti that is the street art of the day and tells a story on the walls of a city and calls forth the people of the street to join the gang…the gang of Christ. The least in the kingdom has become greater than John the Baptist who focused on repentance…The least focuses on grace. The least releases the glory of Jesus and manifestations of Jesus' presence through His healing power. The least may not look presentable or wise.

But wisdom is proved right by her actions.

The actions of Todd challenged me. Indeed, I could not help but examine my own unbelief under the microscope of Jesus, who after commenting on John the Baptist in Matthew 11, began to denounce the cities in which most of his miracles had been performed, because they did not repent. Apparently, the cities that embrace the miracles are the ones that position themselves to receive a lasting revival and ongoing urban transformation.

"Woe to you, Korazin! Woe to you, Bethsaida! If the miracles that were performed in you had been performed in Tyre and Sidon, they would have repented long ago in sackcloth and ashes.

The actions of Todd challenged me to enter into childlike faith - for my own healing...and for an increase in the presence and power of Christ to move in me and through me to touch other lives. If revival doesn't last in my city, I at least want childlike faith and trust in Jesus to last in me.

... At that time Jesus said, "I praise you, Father, Lord of heaven and earth, because you have hidden these things from the wise and learned, and revealed them to little children. Yes, Father, for this was your good pleasure.

I've gone home from Lakeland, yet Todd's actions still stir me to drop the critical nature about things that are beyond my experience and reach up and out for an increase in childlike faith. Only the children can truly receive the hidden things of Jesus and believe the outrageous manifestations of His glory released through healing – Christians and unbelievers alike...freely given, without condition—for this is the father's pleasure, that His children be healed. Healing is scriptural. Power evangelism is scriptural. Seeing angels is scriptural. The strangest insights into the heavenly realm are reserved for little children. The wise and the learned usually miss out.

I went to see a reed swaying in the wind and the glory of God expressed in healing revivals. And I was not disappointed. I saw the glory captured on the expression of a single face that tells the story of a hundred, perhaps a thousand others who have attended the meetings.

Todd stood in the middle of two lines of people flowing past him to receive a touch of anointing oil and impartation for power; joy and passion sparkled in evident delight in his eyes as he prayed for thousands of people moving past. I walked by him and felt the presence of God as his oil-smeared palm lightly touched my forehead. Then I lingered off to the side to watch the others walk by and move back towards their seats.

One elderly man practically skipped through the end of the anointing line pushing a wheelchair with a small crowd of family members trailing behind him. The sheer joy on his face told the whole story as it suddenly dawned on me that the man was pushing the wheelchair that his relatives had brought him in. It held nothing now but a couple of folding chairs that his relatives had been sitting in. Just that one healing, that one glimpse of sheer joy mingling with the glory of God on his elderly face as he pushed his old chair along, was enough for me to believe.

I had seen more than a reed swaying in the wind. I had seen a man, one of hundreds, undeniably healed as a manifestation of the presence of God's love moving during a meeting facilitated by a tattooed and pierced, young holy man.

I had glimpsed the glory of God awakening hearts to a Father who loves us enough to heal us...for *He forgives all of our sins and heals all of our diseases...*
Even yours! Even mine!

--Julia Loren[1]

"That's My Roger!"

Rhonda Martens came to the Outpouring from Omak, Washington, and, like many, volunteered to volunteer. ("Use me, God!") Her assigned post was working at the *Run With Fire Ministries* table, where evangelist musician Roy Fields was making his ministry, music and t-shirts available. Here is her story.

1 juliascribe.blogspot.com. Julia Loren's book, *Shifting Shadows of Supernatural Power*, quotes Todd Bentley. Pastor Bill Johnson is one of the contributing authors.

I traveled with three other women to Lakeland. We arrived on a Thursday. We were in the lobby of our motel checking in when two ladies walked through the lobby and out the door. I felt compelled to ask them if they had been to the revival so I walked after them. Yes, they had. Both were from Canada, one is a pastor. We hit it off right away. They asked us to join them for lunch, but first they had to go to Ignited Church (where this originally broke out) to pick up a CD. That was good since we would know where it was. Then we went to a restaurant close to the church for lunch. I could tell many in there were from the revival...I could just tell by the look on their faces...

...I had been a volunteer at Roy's table, passing out T-shirts. The tag on my shirt said 'Fresh Fire Volunteer.' Some woman probably no taller than 5'2", sporting a shaved head with a Mohawk and wearing a black T-shirt that said "Keep staring, I might do a trick for you," pointed to my volunteer tag and said, "Come here." Well, I'm not going to argue with any woman with a Mohawk. She pointed to the front and said, "We need you on the prayer team."

So I walked up to where many other people were gathering and she barked out another order. We were to line up in front of the stage facing the people. I followed the guy in front of me around to the opposite side of the stage, facing the people, all wanting a touch from God. I felt more qualified passing out T-shirts.

Then the voice from the stage boomed in the microphone and said for people to pick one and make a line in front of that person and they will pray for you. I've never gone through Todd's 'healing and miracle' class. I've never even been to one of his meetings before. But a woman with a Mohawk said, "Come here," so I went, and there I was. People were lining up in front of me to pray for them. "Oh, Jesus...HELP."

The first young woman in 'my line' came up to me and said she needed prayer because she has compulsive behavior. It's very noisy in the tent. So I put my cheek on her cheek and prayed...I asked her name, then told her she was beautiful, that Father was so pleased with her that she didn't have to do anything to 'win' His approval...she already had it. She was crying as I was holding her and speaking into her ear. Words of affirmation. Words of how He loves her, how special she is to Him, and how He is pleased by her. He loves to look at her beautiful face and hear her sweet voice. She's crying. I asked for Heaven to invade her life. For the Kingdom of God to be established in her life...Jesus, just like you prayed and taught us to pray.

The next woman came and said, "I have breast cancer." I didn't have a box of 3x5 cards with specific prayers for specific needs. I only had, "There is no cancer in heaven, God doesn't have cancer; you can't give what you don't have." I invited heaven into her life, and agreed with Jesus and reminded Him of what He prayed...on earth as it is in heaven. For heaven to be released into her life...

Then another woman with a lump on her chest. Again my cheek to her cheek and I prayed the only thing I knew...there is no cancer in heaven and I invited heaven to invade her life.

Then, she stepped aside and there he was...in a wheel chair. His wife pushed his wheel chair up to me. I bent over to ask him how I could pray for him. He mumbled. I couldn't understand because they were not words, just mumbled sound. I looked up at his wife. She said, "He has an inoperable brain tumor." I leaned down to ask him his name. Once again, he mumbled. I looked up in her face and she said, "His name is Roger."

I put my cheek on his cheek and once again prayed the only thing I knew. Jesus you said...you prayed 'on earth as it is in heaven'... there is no cancer in heaven. I invited the Kingdom of God into Roger's life...be healed in Jesus name. I stood up and looked... expecting? I don't know what I was expecting, but I felt more qualified to be passing out T-shirts....

Sunday was our last night at the meetings. Once again, worship was wonderful. I was enjoying His Presence, the music, the atmosphere...the Spirit was glorious.

Then, I looked up on the platform as people were lining up to give glory to God for the miracle they received.

I heard someone ask. "What did Jesus do for you?" and he answered clearly so all could understand, "I had an inoperable brain tumor, and Jesus healed me."

"Sir, what is your name?"

"My name is Roger."

It was the Roger I had prayed for! He had risen from his wheel chair, walked up the steps onto the platform and, standing with his wife by his side, gave glory to God. This time he did not mumble, he spoke so all could hear and understand. No more paralysis on his left side. He was healed and Jesus did it.

Something exploded in me! I was yelling to the women with me... that's Roger, that's the Roger I prayed for. I was trembling, crying, jumping up and down. That's the Roger I prayed for!

I had gone to a revival. I really can't tell you why I went. Was I just curious as to what 'flavor' this one would be? I had been to Toronto and Pensacola. Each was wonderful, each different. Different emphasis. Different expressions of God.

This one IS different. I'm different.

I'd been depressed for the last four years, dry, parched, defeated, easily discouraged, earthly minded. I should have been one of the ones going up to someone in the prayer line. Asking for what? I don't know.

But this I do know. Jesus said, "On earth as it is in heaven." I was touched by heaven. And I don't ever want it to change. I experienced church. Church, where Jesus is welcome, Jesus is lifted up. He drew me into his heart.

I went from passing out T-shirts, to being called by the woman with the Mohawk to get on the prayer team and line up. I prayed for a man in a wheel chair. God healed him of his cancer. He healed me too. My disease was just as destructive...

When Jesus was baptized by John, the Holy Spirit descended and rested on Jesus. But the Holy Spirit remained. My prayer is that with me, He remains. Did I bring back the Fire? Yes. What an honor and privilege, and I remain hungry for *more* of Him.

--Rhonda Martens[2]

A Resurrection From The Dead in Tasmania, Australia:

On Monday the 23rd of June, 2008, in Tasmania, Australia, a man 36 years of age died in the back seat of a car due to a massive heart attack. He is a husband and a father of 4 children. His father-in-law and a close friend were also with him in the car when the event occurred.

On that day, my wife and I, who are in ministry, just happened to pull up in a McDonald's parking lot, when we heard cries for help.

We have been watching the Lakeland revival on God-TV faithfully as our spirits have been lifted and our faith stirred! For some time now we had been crying out for a move of God in Tasmania and the Lord had now begun to move!

We were the first ones on the scene and began to help with CPR as the young man had no pulse or heart beat and his face had turned completely blue. At the same time my wife and I began to pray in other tongues and cried out to God for mercy for this man who was dead or dying.

Thirty minutes later the medics arrived onto the scene. They continued giving CPR, but confirmed that he was dead on arrival. They then proceeded to use the "electric shock paddles" but with no results. They then attempted a second time but there was still no sign of life.

During this time my wife and I were off to the side fervently praying to the Lord for a resurrection from the dead! We then

2 After writing about her experiences, Rhonda returned to Florida twice more, bringing her husband, and another couple to share the Fire. Please see her "Last Word" testimony in Chapter Sixteen.

commanded his spirit to come back into his body in the Name of the Lord Jesus Christ and began to thank the Lord for the answer.

At that time the medics decided to use the electric paddles a third time, which was not something they usually do, we were told later.

But on the third attempt this young man's vital signs suddenly came up!

The young man, "Joe," as I'll call him, was still in very serious condition and later placed in the "High Dependency Unit" at the Royal Hobart Hospital. There, he was put on a "life support machine" and placed also into an induced coma. It was confirmed by doctors that he was clinically dead as only the machines were keeping him alive.

We and others in Tasmania began to pray earnestly for the next several days that the Lord would raise him up for the glory of God!

On Thursday three days later, Joe began to stir in his bed, as he first began to move his hand and then later his knee, up and down. We were told by his wife that Joe just suddenly woke up!

That same day he was taken off the life support machine as well as all the other tubes. He also sat up and began talking to all his family members!! He even made several trips ON HIS OWN to the bathroom that very same day!!

We have spoken to the wife who is unsaved, and as she told us over and over again, "It's a miracle; it's a miracle!!!" We are now planning to visit the family soon to share the good news of Jesus Christ! Our cry is to see revival in the great South land of the Holy Spirit.

--Pastor Anthony Ray Castro, Missionary.

Chapter Two
Early Visions for Lakeland

Nine years ago, while we were still in my father's Carpenter's Home Church, the Lord gave Bishop Clarice Fluitt a vision. For you who aren't familiar with Bishop Clarice, let me tell you, she is the Lord's most outrageous, powerful woman. She simply walks into a room, and electricity sparks off her!

Bishop Clarice and her husband, George, are co-founders of the Eagle's Nest World Prayer and Training Center in Monroe, Louisiana. She moves predominantly and powerfully in the office of a prophet. Blessed with an incredibly authoritative voice, she sings like a strong angel. Wise—she is wise beyond measure. Above all of that, she is utterly sold out to the Kingdom of God.

In 2000, Bishop Clarice came to our church and began to prophecy that there was coming an unprecedented move of the Spirit to our church. She prophesied that the outpouring would bring in those that were "tattooed, pierced, and have green hair!" We had no idea that she was talking about the evangelist.

At that time, the Lord gave her a vision. She saw a *shofar* turned toward the earth, surrounded by a vibrant, emerald-green heaven, and out from the *shofar* rushed a river of green, hot oil. I want to let her tell you about the vision and some of her thoughts about what has happened since:

> The hot, green oil was pouring out onto the earth over discarded burnt stones and the dry bones of those who had died without receiving the fullness of their hopes.
>
> The Lord made me to understand about the discarded burnt stone vision. Whenever man builds a church, there is material that doesn't fit the pattern of the human architect. Perhaps the blueprint called for seven feet of marble, but it came in an eight

foot slab. So the builders throw one foot of the marble into the trash heap. Same quality, same everything, but it just doesn't meet their specifications. In fine homes particularly, excess molding and such, so costly, have to be thrown away. Wonderful things — just thrown away.

But the Divine Architect doesn't throw anything away. God said of those things that were discarded — the dry bones of those who have died in faith, "I am going to pour out green oil upon the face of this earth." I could hear this green oil, which speaks of the anointing and the unction of God, as it came upon the earth. The sound was like when one pours water on hot oil. Very explosive, popping everywhere. Power. The *dunamis* of God.[3]

So when the anointed Word and this oil and water came together, there was an explosion of the *dunamis* power. And the stones and the bones began to shake and rattle, and came together to form what appeared to be a majestic throne of fire. I saw a whirlwind of fire. Our God is a consuming fire, and if He is fire, then we must be the flame of God. So much of this is fresh fire, fresh fire. This fire came like a tornado.

"Behold. I will build a corporate man and he will only have eyes heavenward." A man came out of the fire; he was made of burnt stones and dry bones — those things that had been discarded. I looked at the man; he was golden and on fire. Gold refined to its finest degree is transparent, and as I looked at this man, I could see that every cell in his body was a person. He was composed of billions of cells.

And the Lord said, "Behold, the corporate man. In this hour I will do a new thing." What is that new thing? I could see that it was similar to a caterpillar, making a metamorphosis, a coming out of the cocoon.

So when the anointed Word and this oil and water came together, there was an explosion of the dunamis power...

The Lord said, "The spirit and the soul will marry." Come together

---

3 *Dunamis* is a Greek word that means power, strength, authority, enablement. It is the root word for "dynamite." See Acts 1:8a. "But the Holy Spirit will come upon you and give you **power.** Then you will tell everyone about me in Jerusalem, in all Judea, in Samaria, and everywhere in the world."

under the explosion of the *dunamis* power. Spirit is "male." Soul is "female." And the human body is the dirt that covers the glory of God.

My spirit, a third of me, lives in sinless perfection.

My soul is like the momma who continues to make excuses for the flesh. (Oh, Junior is just tired; he had a bad day.) The soul has allowed misconduct of the body. In Proverbs, it says it is a shameful thing for a slave to rule in the house of the king. The body is never going to vote for God unless it comes under the discipline of the spirit and soul in agreement—a covenant between spirit and soul.

First, the soul must be transformed by the REVEALED word of God—be ye transformed...[4] He that is sanctified and he that becomes sanctified have become one. Once the spirit brings the emotion and it amalgamates with the intellect, then it is a finished work. Then there is immortality.

So God said this metamorphosis of the corporate man will happen in Central Florida. He said it will be seen by the entire world, every eye will know that it is done.

The kingdom of God is the kingdom of the Word. If we agree with God, we will see the manifestation. God does not do things *to* us, as *through* us. We come to an understanding with God that you are healed, you are prosperous...you have all these things, but you have to possess them. Just like when Israel came through the wilderness, and it was the Promised Land, but they had to possess it.

We who are the redeemed can no longer live in that mentality of "do something to me." Something's going to fall on me... Nothing is going to fall any more. Everything is coming UP. If you don't understand the location you will be in a constant state of confusion.

Most significant concept in real estate is location, location,

---

4 Romans 12:2: "And be not conformed to this world: but be **ye transformed** by the renewing of your mind, that ye may prove what is that good, and acceptable, and perfect, will of God." KJV

location. If my location is in Christ, then I can create with Him. Christ has taken our place in heaven; we are to take His place on earth. The dominion of all things has been given to the sons of God. That has not been taught. We've been taught, "If I can get to the pastor or the man of God, then, I can get my miracle, or healing, or whatever..."

So, God said this would take place in an election year. I watched. I saw Barack Obama come out of obscurity in the Democratic campaign with no way to beat the Clinton machine. Yet, he did.

And here was Todd Bentley, coming out of obscurity, highly controversial, with some rowdy friends nobody wanted to associate with. And yet the favor of God was upon him. There was a certain section of the church that wanted to say this was all demonic—but it seems to be of God. People were healed, people were saved, and the name of Jesus was raised up. Thousands and thousands of people came from everywhere.

One pastor called me and asked, "Why would you be a part of that? The revivalists come in and have no care for the local church. They take their money, tear up their buildings, use everybody, and when they leave it's like a swarm of locusts."

I said, "I do know that's how it has happened in the past, but that's not how it's happening here. As an adjunct of Todd's meetings, they are teaching how to evangelize here at Ignited Church, and every day they take two or three hundred people out to witness in the community. And Todd could have, at any moment, taken this whole thing to the tent. But he hasn't. He has been nothing but magnanimous. Any situation that you put under a microscope, you will find an indication of humanity, because we have a treasure in dirt. Don't be amazed if you find some."

I give the word that God gave me. He said, "I will use these people that nobody wants to fool with. Burnt stones. I'm going to do it to irritate the religious traditions of the mind of man. You are a vanguard; you have been created like a little tugboat, not the prettiest thing in the world, but with the motor and the power to pull through the frozen waters of religious tradition and to bring the glory of God behind them.

As I watched the vision, I understood that a fresh epiphany was being released upon the earth for restoring the souls of men. The season for signs and wonders—never known before—was upon us, and it would begin in Florida. The green oil was restoring the burnt stones and dry bones. The Lord said, "Tell my people that I have paid it all, and to return to Father's house."[5]

Bishop Clarice's powerful prophecy was one of many, many visions of this outpouring taking place here in central Florida and in Lakeland—continual, consistent prophesies over many years. So, we should have been ready—or, at least, not surprised. But you know how we are in the human—God's power consistently astounds.

---

5 Interview with Bishop Clarice Fluitt, June 24, 2008

Chapter Three
Digging the Well

Why Here? Why Now? Why Lakeland? Why Ignited?

Before Todd Bentley and his crew trekked down to central Florida from Abbottsford, British Columbia, we were struggling. Ignited Church had about 300 people sitting in a sanctuary designed for 700. Our offices had no furniture. My staff was woefully underpaid. My wife had worked on staff *free* for three years. I personally had not had a raise in 13 years. In fact, I did not even get a raise when I was named senior pastor. We simply could not afford it.

Moneywise, Ignited Church may have been stressed. But in faith, we were tough. In Jesus Christ, we were powerful. Let me tell you why. *We knew this was coming.*

I had preached for over twelve years, since 1996, that this was coming. *We are an apostolic center,* I told our congregation. *We will have church seven days a week. We will be going 24/7. You will have demands placed on you like you have never had before. You will be training and equipping people from all over the world.*

It had been prophesied. Every prophet and apostle who ever came to our church told us that there was coming an outpouring that would touch the nations. That powerful healer, Jim White from Cleveland, Ohio, prophesied several years ago that I was a Holy Ghost arsonist. Fire starter, he said. He told me, "The problem with you is that you are surrounded by fire extinguishers." So he removed them prophetically from my life. It was the very next year that we renamed ourselves: *Ignited Church.* Why ever would I be surprised that we were given "fresh fire?"

But does God give us Outpourings such as this just because we preach it? No. Our minds have to be ready. Our spirits must be prepared, and primed, and willing. Our hearts must hunger and thirst for more and more of God. We must crave, aspire, desire, and yearn for more and more of Jesus. We must dig the well, to be ready for God's time.

My father, Dr. Karl D. Strader, as the senior pastor of Carpenter's Home Church, began "digging the well" here in Lakeland, Florida. Our congregation has known the outpouring of the Spirit, with perhaps a dozen outpourings just like this over the past fifty years. The Jesus Movement, the Hippie Movement, the Latter Rain Movement, the Charismatic Movement, the Prophetic Movement, the Voice of Healing Movement, the Apostolic Movement, the Word of Faith Movement, the Renewal Movement, and many others that you could name—we had it all happening right here in Lakeland!

Long-time church members can tell you what it was like. Highly respected and deeply involved in Carpenter's Home Church and in the life of the Holy Spirit, Dr. Paul and Sofia Williams were members of my father's church for sixteen years before they moved away from the area. Sofia has her own remembrances of their Christian growth and service here.

Sofia's Reflections on the Roots of the Outpouring

> From their earliest days in ministry Pastor Karl and Joyce Strader seemed to have their antennae out, always open to learning what was happening in the greater Body of Christ, and willing to bring it in at Carpenter's. For a pastor and wife to be open to so many streams of God seemed amazing to me. And it has greatly impacted my life as a Christian.
>
> Marilyn Hickey, Richard Roberts, Francis McNutt, Dennis and Rita Bennett, Rodney Howard-Browne—the pulpit was open to all these people, so we really got a sense of what was going on in the Body of Christ. Father Francis McNutt was one of the first Roman Catholic priests to be involved in charismatic renewal, and he became hugely respected for his work in the power of the Holy Spirit to transform lives, and for his healing ministry. And he was here in Lakeland, teaching.
>
> I remember, too, meeting Dennis and Rita Bennett. Father Dennis was a heroic Episcopal priest, who took great criticism when he stood up in the pulpit and announced he had received his own personal baptism with the Spirit. Dennis was influential

in the charismatic movement, and I was in training sessions and conferences at Carpenter's when the Bennett's came and taught us about inner healing—how to get people healed of things they were dealing with from their past.

Many things that we now accept and appreciate caused a great deal of controversy back then. When sacred dance started to become part of worship, I was part of the worship team. The Straders had to treat it with great wisdom. They had paid a price for moving into this area because there was limited openness for it in the Assemblies of God at that time. Worship Dance was initially introduced to our congregation through children.

My daughter, Debbie, and her friend, Nanette, were twelve or thirteen years old and were anointed and quite talented in movement. Many times in a morning service they would do a choreographed piece or simply just express worship spontaneously in movement to music beautifully. It was a demonstration that God could use this kind of expression to draw us closer and to open our spirits to Him. Their intimacy with the Lord is what came through and touched people in a powerful way.

The Straders encouraged all giftings in the Body of Christ. It was risky business to validate these gifts, but Pastor Strader was willing to follow the leading of the Holy Spirit. We even had power teams using their gifts of strength to present the gospel.

When Karl Strader began to move into deliverance, he was greatly criticized. Even the role of intercessors in the church was groundbreaking. Now, we hardly think about that at all, but at one time, it was not a role that was being recognized.

Some things I didn't understand. I had to ask the Holy Spirit to show me what it all meant. Like Holy laughter—this was one of the major manifestations during the Rodney Howard-Browne meetings.

Rodney's ministry was catapulted throughout the world in the mid 1990's at Carpenter's. I never thought I could be in church for six, seven or eight hours at a time! Sometimes we'd get home at 2 or 3:00 a.m. We would be in the meetings, just open to what the Holy

Spirit was doing.

I remember one service in particular. Thousands wanted Rodney to pray for them. Lines of people stretched around the sanctuary, then out the doors and around the grounds just laughing in the Spirit. I had begun to realize that the laughter was the manifestation of the touch of God on the lives of people who were hungry for Him.

The services of the various outpourings were broadcast throughout the years by radio and television. Many lives were impacted around the world. There was so much we recieved from all these streams of God's supernatural visitations.[6]

Dr. Rodney Howard-Browne came to Carpenter's Home Church in 1993. That was the biggest one: a revival movement that helped trigger the Toronto Blessing in Canada, the Brownsville Revival in Pensacola, Florida, and new revivals in New Zealand, and Australia, and parts all over the world—through what happened right here in Lakeland in 1993.

But Rodney Howard-Browne kept saying over and over again, "This is just the tip of the iceberg! This is just the beginning. And what is about to happen is going to happen at an accelerated pace."

Well, we all just thought that was an evangelist's "thing." But it has happened at an accelerated rate, just as he prophesied. And he continues to preach that there is a great end-time outpouring that will sweep millions into the Kingdom of God.

Our congregation continued to cry out for this "coming revival" or "outpouring" of God's Spirit. Because such an incredible well had been dug, our hearts were ready for something huge. We were ready—we thought....

Bishop Clarice Fluitt puts it this way:

One of the Biblical principles that helps us to understand the outpouring of God's presence and power is the principle of praise and worship. Inspired praise and worship will ignite a dimension of corporate agreement that will demand a biblical response between God and man. Remember, Judah is the plow of God (Hosea 10:11:

6 Interview with Sofia Williams, 7/25/2008

Judah shall plow, and Jacob shall break his clods.) Inspired praise serves as a digging instrument that breaks the fallow ground of the human soul.

Mankind is composed of dirt, and dirt will grow whatever is planted. When we praise and worship God corporately with abandonment and surrender our will corporately, we spiritually dig a hole that must have a divine deposit or revelation that agrees with the depth of our praise and worship. Consider: if you dig a 10-foot hole and only plant a tiny, immature seed, your seed will not reproduce what produced it. It will be smothered because of the *depth* of the digging.

The church is learning how to transplant mature things into the deep praise and worship that releases glory. It is the season that we must see from God's view. Whenever God creates, His pattern is always to create mature.

That is what happened here. Collectively, we had dug an enormous hole, and God had just the full-blown, mature thing to fill it! Our church should have been prepared for it. If we weren't, it was our own fault! But having said all that, nobody could have been prepared for *this*! We literally had to lay our lives down. Period. Mind-boggling. We were prepared for a tidal wave. We were *not* prepared for a tsunami! And this has been a tsunami. There is no way to prepare for a tsunami. It is impossible. All you can do is hunker down and wait until it is over, then clean up the mess! You just have to deal with whatever happens.

Chapter Four
Honor Thy Parents

As you can probably tell, I am inordinately proud of my parents. I love and honor them very much. It is important for people to know that my parents paid a steep, painful price for digging this well so that, today, God could do this mighty work here.

Back in the 1960's, my father, Karl Strader took a church that seated about 700, but had only about 350 people attending. Ten years later, it had grown to 2,000. My father built a church on downtown Main Street that seated 1,800. By the 1980's, there were about 4,000 people who called my father's church their church home! We were running five services a Sunday to accommodate the crowds. As you might guess, we were looking for a bigger place.

There was a plot of land, over 700 acres, just north of Lakeland's city limits. Sitting on it was the Carpenter's Home, a union-owned Mediterranean-style structure built in 1929 (the same year that my father was born) where three or four hundred retired carpenters lived. By the time we started looking at the property, the home had closed down because its residents had either passed away or moved. It had sat empty for about seven years and, of course, was up for sale. We bought it, and promptly began planning a 10,000-seat sanctuary. In 1985, we moved into the new facility, changed the name of the church to Carpenter's Home Church, and began to renovate the older structure for an educational building.

Carpenter's Home Church was a trans-denominational church, a focal point for the Charismatic move of God, which had begun its up-swing in the mid-1960's. At the time we moved into Carpenter's Home, that Charismatic Flow was at its peak. The church quickly grew to nearly 7,000 constituents.

About 1987, only a couple of years later, the Charismatic movement began to wane. At the same time, several television personalities in the Christian world began to have severe problems in their personal lives. Almost every one of these people had helped in a year-long dedication of our facility. We experienced a formidable backlash. Our congregation became restless. Certain people came against my Dad and Carpenter's Home Church.

Psychologists tell us that someone who is accusing publicly is usually at fault about the same thing. In the 1980's we had one famous television evangelist accusing another famous television evangelist of sinful excesses, while he himself was involved in sexual impurities. We've seen time and again, that when one minister is accusing another minister publicly of some great crime or impropriety, we find out, sometimes years later, that they were culpable of the same thing. That's why we have to be very careful in publicly accusing somebody. Are we ourselves guilty? The scary thing is: sometimes we are not even aware that we are harboring the same guilty thoughts or actions. Humble self-examination is key before we dare to accuse.

Because of all this turmoil, there came an out-and-out insurrection. In 1989, one-third of the congregation left the church and scattered to other existing churches, and even a new church was formed practically across the street. Their departure left us with $100,000 in monthly payments. We never missed a payment, but we did have to refinance, plus we had to sell assets, including our radio station, WCIE, which broadcast contemporary Christian music out as far as 70 miles from Lakeland. It was a very difficult time.

In 1993, however, we experienced that glorious move of God with Rodney Howard-Browne. It was a revival that reached around the world in influence. It looked like we would be able to recoup some of our losses.

Then, in 1995, our church took another hurricane-like hit. My brother, Daniel, went to prison for 45 years. More than 200 newspaper articles blitzed the area, in addition to blanket television coverage. Dan had come on economic hard times, and his investment business was said to have violated securities laws involving about 65 people and three million dollars. Because our father was a prominent pastor in this comparatively small town of 70,000 people, the media and the devil had a heyday.

Finally, in 2005, because of my father's age—and with a desire to protect my parents' health—adjustments had to be made. Shane Simmons, my brother-in-law, and I desired to carry on the work. We could not do so in that mammoth, 10,000-seat auditorium.

Church Without Walls of Tampa, said to be the second-largest church congregation in America, purchased the complex. In the process, our congregation gained a 3,000-seat church in Auburndale, about 20 minutes away from Lakeland. Part of the congregation went to Auburndale, others stayed in Lakeland.

As you know, I am senior pastor of the Lakeland church, called *Ignited*. Shane is the senior pastor at *Life Church* in Auburndale, Florida. And Dad's *Carpenter's Home Church* continues to exist under the name, *Carpenter's Home International Internet Church*. For much of 2007 and 2008, he recorded over 40,000 hits on his website each month. He is fond of saying, "One thing I do know, *if I don't blow it*: God has given me an opportunity in my retirement days, because of modern technology, to reach more people in the next five or ten years than all my fifty plus years of ministry put together!"

Much to my joy, Dad periodically preached at the Outpouring, at morning services and at the ministers' seminars. I think it gave him a new lease on life. And that was why it was so cool to have my Dad standing next to me in front of the whole world in the Apostolic Alignment ceremony on June 23, 2008. Dad and I stood side by side, shoulder to shoulder. We were re-digging Dad's wells.

Remember the story of Isaac re-digging the wells of his father? Isaac went down to Gerar, the land of the Philistines, and King Abimelech gave him permission to live there.

Isaac planted crops in that land and took in a huge harvest. God blessed him. The man got richer and richer by the day until he was very wealthy. He accumulated flocks and herds and many, many servants, so much so that the Philistines began to envy him. They got back at him by throwing dirt and debris into all the wells that his father's servants had dug back in the days of his father Abraham, clogging up all the wells.

Then King Abimelech made him leave. He was getting too big, the king said; he was annoying the locals.

So Isaac left. He camped in the valley of Gerar and settled down there. Isaac dug again the wells which were dug in the days of his father Abraham but had been clogged up by the Philistines after Abraham's death....[7]

Perhaps some thought my father was too big. I don't know. The Philistines came and filled in my father's wells with dirt and stones and debris—and it shattered him. Nonetheless, all of those great moves of God were in wells that my father dug. And, once you get out the dirt and stones, you have the original well.

So Isaac re-dug the wells of his father. That is what I did, too. And this Outpouring flooded, saturated, spilled through those wells. And gushed forth blessings to the entire world.

---

7 Genesis: 12-17. (The Message)

Chapter Five
Encountering a Tattooed Evangelist

For several years, we had been reading the stories and articles and listening to the recordings of Todd Bentley. We tried for years to connect with him and invite him to come. Once, I was even able to get his cell phone number and talk with him, but he didn't know me from a stump. He later used me in a sermon illustration when speaking about "hunger and desperation." He told his audience, "I don't know how this pastor got my cell phone number, but he sure was desperate for God!" And I was. And I still am.

Apparently, that desperation for God clicked with him. In June of 2007, a day or so before my birthday, I got a call that Todd was coming to central Florida for a conference. Would I like to have him speak for one night before his conference began?

"It would be the best birthday present you could give me." Todd came, with less than two weeks' notice, and we packed out the building. We developed an instant relationship, and I invited him to come back the following year.

In October of 2007, Bobby Sullivan, one of Todd's associate evangelists, spoke at Ignited Church. During those meetings, we sensed something shift in the heavenlies. Something awesome was about to happen, and we *felt* it. On April 2, 2008, just six months later, Todd began the five-day Signs and Wonders Conference in our church.

Expectation was very high. In Australia, two weeks before, the New Zealand prophet Rob Deluca had prophesied a coming anointing on Todd that would boomerang around the world in four strategic regions. The boomerang would double in force once it came to central Florida, he said. Rob even mentioned the Lakeland revival of 1993. He had no idea that Todd was headed to the very congregation that experienced that revival.

Needless to say, we all went crazy with excitement. We knew that something special was about to happen. But we had NO IDEA the magnitude of what Holy Spirit was planning.

That first Wednesday night was explosive. The building was comfortably filled. But something in my spirit had already told me to prepare for overflow crowds. We had wired both the children's and youth rooms with closed circuit. This enabled us to spread out from the sanctuary with 700 seats, to over 1300 with the two overflow rooms. We'd also wired the outside patio, which could seat an additional 400. The second night we filled the first overflow room.

The holy energy was unprecedented. The hair on our arms literally stood straight up as the very atmosphere was charged with the electricity of God. Incredible miracles began to flow. Even Todd seemed taken aback with the ease of the miracles. We both conduct overseas crusades and often see great miracles…but not in America. Not like this!

The third night, as Todd walked into the room, our eyes met in a jubilant, expectant look. Standing on the front row, with music and praise flowing all about us, I told him, "I think we need to go another week."

He laughed. "I just told my staff, 'I think we need to talk with Pastor Stephen about going another week.'" We announced it that night.

Every service took us another huge step *up* into the anointing. I can't explain it any other way. The crowds filled both overflows. By Sunday, we had to lock the doors because the fire marshal required us to limit the capacity to 1,300. We had hundreds outside the building on the patio, and often turned hundreds away. We began looking for larger facilities. People lined up as early as 3:00 o'clock in the afternoon, just as they had at the Brownsville Revival in Pensacola.

My brother-in-law, Pastor Shane Simmons at Life Church in Auburndale, Florida, pastors a 3,000-seat facility about twenty minutes away. He graciously opened his doors to us. And we overflowed his building and had to turn hundreds away! The Outpouring promptly moved into the 8,000-seat Lakeland Center Arena—and we filled that up. We relocated to the Tigers Baseball Stadium that seats 10,000 with a grassy knoll overlooking left field that could seat another 2,000. We filled the whole thing. Then we went to the Lakeland Airport at the Sun-N-Fun Campground and did an open air meeting with over 12,000. There was a traffic jam, and the police told us that literally thousands were blocked from getting into the campground for miles down the road.

The first three to four weeks were totally consumed with finding facilities. We finally came up with the idea of the tents – a clear span structure – as a semi-permanent home. Two massive vinyl tents were attached – side by side – and could hold 10,000. If you hadn't actually been to one of the meetings, it is hard to envision. In your mind's eye you might picture old canvas tents, hot and dusty. These, however, were air conditioned and quite comfortable. What a treat to look up during a Florida thunderstorm and be able to see the dimples in the vinyl roof as the rain pelted down. That often prompted the worship leader to break into the song, "Rain Down," and people would cheer. (Unless, of course, a rain drop sneaked through and plopped on the top of your head. Even that made people laugh. It was all a part of the total experience.)

Amazingly, about 50% of the crowd lived outside the state of Florida, and 40% lived outside the USA. Every night, we would announce each country represented, and people cheered. Each meeting had people from dozens of different countries—Canada, England, France, Spain, the Netherlands, the Ukraine, South Korea, Norway, Sweden, the Philippines, and on and on and on. Once, we even had a person from North Korea. They were drawn, of course, by the power of the Presence of God that they saw broadcast on God-TV and on our webcasts. It was above and beyond anything we ever imagined.

The Unprecedented Webcasts

About the first or second day into the Outpouring, one of my computer-savvy tech guys came to me and said, "Pastor, do you know that we could actually broadcast this on the internet?"

"What are you talking about? How much would it cost?" He told me it wouldn't cost a cent. That was a *very* good price. We decided to put the meeting on the web, just to see what it looked like. But we didn't even have a proper camera—I had a simple home digital camera, so we used that. To let people know, I sent out an email to the fewer than 2,000 people on our church's email list. That night, five hundred people logged in to my home video camera, sitting in the back of the room, on a wide shot! The first night!

I immediately borrowed a better camera.

Daily, the count went up—800, 1,000, 1,200, 1,800, growing quickly to over 2,000. Our internet provider, *uStream*, counts IP addresses, which are like fingerprints for a computer. Within three weeks of being on the webcast, a quarter of a million different computers had actually logged on! By the time we reached about fifty days, we had already topped one million.

By the sixtieth or sixty-fifth day, people had discovered God-TV's telecasts and were now tuning in—or were logging on to Fresh Fire, which was re-broadcasting the telecast. God-TV began to drain away most of Ignited Church's webcasts. So we turned our attention to an area that *wasn't* being covered. Ignited purchased television equipment and joined a new webcast company, *iWorshiphere.com,* using their services to broadcast the morning sessions, with viewership ranging from 2,000 to 8,000 daily.

God-TV continued to broadcast the night services, with about 50,000 more watching online. The amazing thing is that *those* 50,000 a day were merely on the website. There were **millions** more watching on God-TV! Nobody even knows what those numbers were. It could have been two million, it could have been thirty million; there was no way of knowing how many were tuned in.

How did the God-TV connection come about?

Todd had a long-term relationship with God-TV. In 2007, when he had scheduled a three-day meeting in Orlando, God-TV planned for months in advance to broadcast live. Then, when Todd came back for the Signs and Wonders Conference, he advised God-TV that he was coming. They had it in the back of their minds that if we videotaped it, they might use one or two nights of it someplace--but they had not put it on their schedule.

Jeffrey Levinson, from God-TV here in the region, came just to enjoy the conference. But he met with Todd after the first night's meeting. "Man! We've got to videotape this! This is wild!" They brought the truck here the second weekend, and started videotaping. Those videotapes were jetted overnight to New York, where they were edited and sent by fiber optic to Jerusalem. Then they were put on the transmitter and up-linked to the fifteen satellites that cover the world. They did all of that in twenty-four hours. They did that three nights in a row. It boggles the mind, logistically.

Because of the response from those three nights, God-TV immediately took us live. We were live for well over a hundred days, because the response was so incredible. And the Outpouring was beamed nightly into homes in 214 countries. From Jerusalem!

Prayer Requests Clog the Server!

One time--*one time!*—Todd put on the television screen a brand new email address for prayer requests, prayer@ignitedchurch.com. Within seconds, our computer went, "Ding." Then, "Ding... Ding... Ding." Then, "Dingd ingdingdingdingdingding...." Within minutes we were getting 100 emails a minute.

For twenty-four solid hours we got a hundred emails a minute! We finally had to cut off that particular email address and put up another one, because the first server was totally overloaded! It is fixed now, thank God, and you may again send prayer requests to prayer@ignitedchurch.com.

At one time, I had over 60,000 emails on my computer that I hadn't had time to read! Todd routinely came over nightly and laid hands on my computer and prayed over the prayer requests. I did, as well—I often had my laptop open on the platform, journaling the meeting. Prayer requests would come in during the service, and I would be able to pray over them immediately.

We now have our prayer teams praying over the prayer requests as they come in each day. I read them as I can. But I don't worry about not being able to read them all before prayer; Jesus knows what the needs are. I trust the Lord to take them.

Not Just a Nighttime Outpouring:
Outpouring Morning Services at Ignited Church—Sunday through Friday!

Mornings, it was fun to drive through our packed-out parking lot. Clumps of people would be huddled, praying, right there on the tarmac. Others would be scurrying to get in line. Some were driving through, nervously trying to find a place to park.

Then, there were the placards. On one car with California plates I saw a hand-colored sign that boldly decreed, "Lakeland or bust!" It was a very different kind of gold rush!

If you didn't get to come down here for the Outpouring, you may have thought that the only things going on in Lakeland were the night services at the tent. You couldn't have been more wrong. People were trekking here from all over the world to get some, and we wanted to be absolutely sure they were filled to the brim when they went home.

So, every morning, from Sunday to Friday, (we took Saturdays off to deep-clean the church and make it sacred for the next week's worship) we offered morning services. These were more intimate than the evening meetings, only having 700 people or more, instead of 10,000. We received many testimonies from people who found that they were touched more by the morning services than the evening meetings. That doesn't mean one was better than the other, of course. It just means that people have different needs at different times when it comes to their worship. It was our honor to be an integral part of that.

Friday Morning Ministers' Seminars

By Friday, people started to pour into Lakeland for the weekend. Friday morning services began overflowing the overflow rooms! So we decided to be sneaky, and offer a ministers' seminar at Pastor Wayne Friedt's Believers' Fellowship church nearby. There was method in our madness. It gave us more room in the Ignited service, and allowed us to offer a different kind of spiritual food for the ministers. It was more intimate even than the Ignited services, and we could give sermons directed at meeting their needs.

Street Evangelism: Personal Power Evangelism

Some fathers of the faith sat down with us and pointed out that one of the marks of an outpouring is that souls are being saved and that you are impacting the city where it is happening.

It was already in our spirit to have street evangelism. The wonderful evangelist and musician Roy Fields, who often ministered at the Outpouring, conducts his revivals at night and street evangelism during the day, wherever he goes. Evangelist Rodney Howard-Browne, we discovered, starts street evangelism training in every revival he does.

We found Jeff Lewis, a young man who had attended one of Rodney's schools and who now has his own evangelism ministry, "Citytaker Ministries." Fresh Fire hired him full time. At the same time, Ignited Church hired Jeff's wife, Melanie Lewis, to coordinate with the Lakeland Alliance of Ministers who were working together to follow up on the new converts.

Six days a week, Jeff and Melanie and their teachers trained people to do street evangelism. Everybody who came to the Outpouring (everybody who was *willing!*) came to a sixty-to-ninety-minute training session. Then, we sent them out on the streets. Jeff and Melanie helped us train over 12,000 people before Jeff launched out across the USA to share the Outpouring.

"The whole Body of Christ must be evangelistic," Jeff Lewis said, "and God has given us the tools to do it. We teach on subjects such as boldness, healing the sick, Words of Knowledge, miracles, taking a city, the Power of One, and wanting fruit that will remain. After teaching, we demonstrate! In the training, people have been healed: spinal stenosis for 31 years, plugged ducts in the jaw, tumors disappearing, and much, much more."

Street Evangelism is more than the street

Not everybody goes to the streets. But they do use their techniques when they go into a restaurant, or a gas station, or the convenience store, or the pharmacy, or the barber shop. I like to call it personal power evangelism.

It isn't about taking a specific time to go out evangelizing. This is a daily walk. For me, I always start the morning by praying, "Give me divine encounters and divine witness today, Lord." Then, perhaps I'll be walking through the grocery store and I see a lady who's obviously in pain. Perhaps she has her arm in a sling, or a brace on a foot. *If I feel led to do so by the Holy Spirit*, I say, "I notice your arm is in a sling. Are you in pain right now?

And she says, "Yes."

"Well, I'm a believer, and I believe that when I pray, Jesus will heal your arm. Would you like for me to pray for your arm?" And when I pray and it is healed, I am given the perfect opportunity to lead her to the Lord.

That, in a nutshell, was—and is—the principle of our street evangelism. If you are interested in knowing more about street evangelism training, the logical, easy-to-use course is available at Jeff's website. Please utilize it for the glory of Jesus.[8]

Therefore, go and make disciples of all nations, baptizing them in the name of the Father and of the Son and of the Holy Spirit! Matthew 28:19 (NIV)

New Believers' Classes:

Every day, people were born again on the streets. The street evangelists were encouraged to get their names, addresses, and phone numbers, and bring them to the service that night. Then, later, when we did an official altar call, the people were brought forward and taken to the side where they filled out salvation—or decision—reports.

One night, for example, there were fifty-seven people who responded in the altar call. Out of those, only about half of them were really decisions for the Lord. The others were either rededicating their lives to the Lord, or felt that they needed extra prayer. So, instead of fifty-seven, there were twenty-five. Out of that twenty-five, four were from the Lakeland area; everybody else was an hour or more away.

I took them all to the side and told them—all of them, no matter where they came from, "Make sure that in the next 24 hours you tell somebody who is in significant spiritual leadership in your life that you have made a rededication or recommitment to the Lord tonight. Call your pastor or a friend, or somebody who has spiritual influence in your life. Your responsibility is to tell *somebody* in the next 24 hours.

"Second of all," I said, "in the next seven days, read the Book of John. Anybody who doesn't have a Bible, raise your hand." And we passed out Bibles to those who needed them.

By the end of that particular week, there were approximately 120 people who were legitimate converts who lived within thirty minutes of our church.

---

8 http://www.citytaker.com. Jeff Lewis has his entire evangelism class available on his website. Here is a link for a wonderful testimony: http://www.youtube.com/watch?v=7jSGi_yKIbQ.

They were either truly new converts, or people who had backslidden and were coming back to the Lord and needed discipleship. Out of that 120, twelve chose to come to church. Many migrated back to churches in the area where they had some kind of roots. A few made Ignited their church home. We have welcomed all with open hearts and thanksgiving.

But you will receive power when the Holy Spirit has come upon you; and you shall be My witnesses both in Jerusalem, and in all Judea and Samaria, and even to the remotest part of the earth. Acts 1:8 (NASB)

Chapter Six
Hit By the Tsunami

I could convey what effect the Outpouring had on the Lakeland area in two ways. I could go to the Chamber of Commerce and point out, "We brought millions of dollars into the economy here in Polk County." And that is absolutely true. Every hotel, car rental, restaurant, grocery store—everything was economically blessed by the outpouring.

As far as affecting the local *churches* as a whole, I was disappointed. Less than 1% in either service—day or night—were from the local Lakeland area. That is the opposite of what we experienced in 1993. Then, 60 to 70% of the people coming to the meetings were within an hour's drive. I don't know if there was anything else we could have done to change that, other than being out on the streets, witnessing, which we were.

I think from a practical standpoint, one of the problems was the sheer logistics. The services went from 7:00 to midnight, and people had to work. They may have come to a meeting, then not have come back for two or three weeks. On the other hand, people in my congregation who do work full time jobs were frequently at the tent three and four nights a week, because they had a passion to be there.

I am saddened that more of the people of Lakeland were not impacted by coming to a service. Few pastors from the greater Lakeland area bothered to come to the meetings. Or they came incognito—slipping in, slipping out, and I didn't know that they were there. I do know they were watching.

The good news is that here and there, people began to accept us. One local pastor who had spoken out against the Outpouring recanted. He actually told his congregation: I was wrong, I shouldn't have said anything. I'm not endorsing what is happening, but if you choose to go, it is all right. You need to hear from God for yourself; it doesn't matter who the preacher is.

A couple of months into the Outpouring, I went to a funeral of a high level leader in the Assemblies of God. Dozens and dozens of denominational friends and co-laborers came up afterwards and encouraged me. Shook my hand and said, "We're watching. We're watching every night." So there was that pulse that people were watching on the webcast or on God-TV, rather than physically coming to the tent.

There were two local churches that were dynamically affected by the Outpouring—Believers Fellowship with Pastors Wayne & Matti Friedt and TLC Family Church with Pastors Shirley and Steve Arnold. But whether or not the other churches in town were being affected, the people of the city certainly were. It was a contagious atmosphere. Wal-Mart, restaurants, hotels, grocery stores—wherever you went, people were talking about the Outpouring, talking about Jesus.

It seemed like I couldn't go anywhere. One Sunday afternoon, we walked into the Chinese buffet. And the waitress said, "Oh, you very famous man! You preacher! You preacher! You famous man!" It made me laugh.

One afternoon, I took my daughter to get a new cell phone. The clerk left her customer, came over to me and whispered, "Would you please pray for my friend?" So we did. Right there in the shop.

It happened all over the city. Bishop Clarice Fluitt tells about her experiences while in Lakeland:

> In restaurants, shops, and even on the streets, people were positively talking about the Outpouring. While I was in my hotel I spoke to a maintenance man. I asked him, "Well, have you been to the Fresh Fire revival?" He smiled and said, "No, but I have surely heard a lot of people talking about it."
>
> I began to share some of my observations, and he immediately responded with deep emotion. "Lady, while you are talking, the hair is standing on the back of my arms. You're the third person today that told me I need to go. Tonight, I am going to go to that meeting."
>
> I was meeting a group of ministry colleagues at TGI Friday's for lunch after the morning session, and there were many people there who had been to the morning meeting. The atmosphere in the

restaurant was conducive to experience the power and presence of God. Everyone appeared excited about the Lord.

One lady came over to my table and said, "I just bought all your CD's. Would you sign them, please?" I felt like a penny waiting for change. But I did sign them.

We had the opportunity to visit with a kind couple from Texas with a church on the Rio Grande. "We're just so excited about taking the fire back." They asked me to pray for them. I said, "Well, such as I have, I impart it to you." The next thing I know, from across the room I heard, "Oh, my God! Oh, my God!" The woman I had just prayed for had started witnessing to a waitress whose leg was in a brace, knee to ankle, from a car wreck. She was telling the waitress, "That woman over there (pointing to me) just imparted the anointing to me, and it's transferable! So I'm going to agree with you that your leg is healed." The waitress' leg was instantly healed. She then took off her brace and began to walk without any pain or limitations. God was showing out right in the middle of everyone's lunch!

This was not just an isolated incident. It was happening everywhere. Only those with very limited comprehension could say, "This is of the devil." Everyplace we went people were talking about Jesus. They're full of hope...[9]

How did it affect Ignited Church?

War is hell; people are going to get shot. People are going to get wounded. And some will die. That's what a war does. It blows things up. The Bible says it this way: "Everything that can be shaken, will be shaken."[10]

Hopefully, in my congregation, we "lost" few, because they were prepared for war. They were prayed up. They were spiritually ready. We have tried to call every single person in the congregation, and in all the phone calls we discovered no problems. Not one.

One of the apostles asked during the height of the Outpouring, "How is your church responding to this?" And I told him, "We are in 100% agreement."

9, Interview with Bishop Clarice Fluitt, 6/24/2008
10 Hebrews 12:27

I got critical emails from other people, but not from my congregation. Not one of the leadership, not one of our congregation, not even one fringe person from the congregation expressed that they were unhappy.

There were casualties, I admit. When you are in an outpouring it is easier to drop the ball. You miss somebody in the hospital or sick at home because the pastor could no longer touch the sheep as he could prior to a revival or an outpouring. You are in church every morning from 10:00 to 1:00, and every evening from 7:00 to midnight. It is physically impossible to do *everything*.

As far as my responsibilities as senior pastor goes, my function temporarily shifted. Daily, there were national and international leaders phoning, emailing or text messaging, wanting my attention immediately. I needed to respond immediately. *For a season*, I had to let the other pastors and the elders take personal care of the congregation.

I was totally focused on the role our church was playing in the Outpouring. I was responsible for the morning services and, generally, I felt a responsibility for the overall spiritual life of the Outpouring.

But, after 80 days, I began reintegrating myself back into the life of the church by starting Wednesday night services again. I started speaking, but not preaching. My congregation was getting enough preaching. On Wednesday nights I shared, from my heart, Scripture that would help them understand what they were going through during this Outpouring. The conflicts they were enduring within their own family and friends—those that loved the outpouring; those that hated the outpouring. How to deal with offenses. The hurt of seeing their pastor ridiculed on the internet. And I let them know when we had a victory. I told them the good, the bad and the ugly.

Too Sick to go to the Healing Meetings!

A couple of months into the Outpouring I started taking Saturdays off. I didn't come to the building, and I didn't go to the tent. And I *wanted* to go to the tent. But I didn't. I usually ended up turning on the computer and watching the service in the background while I was preparing my Sunday morning sermon. But I only started taking Saturdays eight weeks in. I was working seven days a week. It wasn't foolish; it just lacked wisdom! I think foolishness would have been to go more than 56 days without a day off!

It did cost me. I spent two days in bed. I couldn't have gone to the tent had I wanted to. Everyone on Fresh Fire staff and everyone on my staff got sick, at one point or another. Because of the fatigue, some flu bug hit us all hard. The common joke was, "We are too sick to come to the healing meetings!"

Mother Theresa

I want to tell you about Mother Theresa. Her real name is Theresa Carder, but we call her Mother Theresa. I know those of you who watched the Outpouring on God-TV know exactly who I'm talking about. She is the blond lady who laid the modesty cloths over those slain in the Spirit on the platform. People came up at the meetings and treated her like a celebrity. It was very humbling to her. She is a member of Ignited Church, and volunteered at *all* those evening meetings.

But here, I'll let her tell her own story:

> People ask me how I came about doing the modesty cloths. I do it at Ignited with several other ladies. We are called the Cover Girls of Ignited Church!
>
> Nobody else was coming to the evening meetings on a regular basis. That's kind of how it came about. So soon they *expected* me to be there! I came every night except once. And I am going to take tomorrow night off. I don't get paid. I'm doing this for Jesus.
>
> I do have to hold myself back a little. There is such an anointing on the stage that sometimes it is hard to stand up. One time I told them, don't throw the cloth at me because I will fall down. They didn't believe me. One of the dignitaries on the platform took a cloth and threw it at me. I fell right into the seats. I got up and said, 'I told you so.' I usually stand towards the back so I can get out of it a little bit, just so I can keep functioning.
>
> That heavy anointing is, of course, one of the great parts about being up there. You can get healed without even asking! At one session at Ignited, my wrist had been hurting so badly, it was hard

to pick up the cloths. Just putting my finger and thumb together would shoot pain halfway up my arm. All I could do was to keep rubbing it. Every time I picked up a cloth, it hurt. That went on for about four days. Then, one night, I got really engrossed in the preaching. I was doing the cloths, and suddenly, I thought, 'Hey! My wrist doesn't hurt." It was just healed!

When people come up to me, sometimes they say, "Oh, we so admire you." The first time they did that I was embarrassed, because I'm not doing it for any praise. It makes you think about your life and how you are living it. First of all, we represent Christ. And secondly, I represent Ignited. If I say something wrong, how will that reflect on what I am doing, what I am showing? I am so conscious of it. So it has changed my life.

If you are hungry for God, you are going to get it here. If a regular church service goes half an hour people start getting antsy. But here, we worship two hours or more, every night. Before we do anything else! When I watch these people singing, "Holy, holy," it makes me cry. It reminds me of the four and twenty elders up there, and how they sing, "Holy, holy, holy," over and over. It reminds me of being in heaven where we'll be able to praise him forever.

I am so thankful. I was born and raised in the church. But still I am far from perfect. But here I am, with all my imperfections, and You still loved me so much, You gave Your son.[11]

Fresh Fire—in charge!

One of the unique aspects of this outpouring is that Todd's ministry—Fresh Fire—was in charge from day one. Let me explain. Because the whole outpouring began during the Fresh Fire Signs and Wonders Conference, Fresh Fire remained in charge. They were responsible for the finances and the platform. While I continued to host the morning services at Ignited Church, I was only delegated the responsibility under their guidelines. They gave me several opportunities to speak each week, but the remainder of the speakers were assigned by them.

Todd and I only met together about three times during the entire

---

11   Interview with Theresa Carter, 6/26/2008

outpouring. Most of my communication was through his staff. The rest of my communication with Todd was by the occasional text message or a brief hello on the platform. Todd's staff was always gracious to me and embraced many of my suggestions and ideas. One of my suggestions was the introduction of both the Leadership and Pastoral Workshops. Several of my colleagues have chastised me for giving up so much control, but I felt I did exactly what the Holy Spirit prompted me to do. I have no regrets or second thoughts.

Where did the money go?

What I did with Fresh Fire before they even came here was to come to an agreement of what it cost me on a day-by-day basis. It would cost this many dollars extra for electricity, cleaning, and for overtime hours. My audio guys, who normally only work Sundays and on Wednesday nights, were now going to work Monday morning, Monday night, Tuesday morning, Tuesday night, etc. And we were going to go five days. (Or so we thought!)

My agreement with Fresh Fire was that they would reimburse us for all of our out-of-pocket expenses, so it didn't cost us financially to have the outpouring. My staff doubled, then tripled, and my expenses doubled. But all of it was covered.

A few weeks in, the Outpouring had to move to a larger facility. The morning services continued in my church, so Fresh Fire gave me the morning offerings. I turned around and returned to them a portion of the offerings as a love gift—because the people were coming to the morning services because of what Fresh Fire was doing at night. The morning offerings have been a great blessing.

We have used the abundance to complete our office furniture—we had *no* office furniture!—and to finish the building with some technical equipment—projectors, television screens, audio equipment, that we had always wanted and couldn't afford. With the additional funds, we have added a children's pastor to the staff, which we had desperately wanted.

Some of our staff were significantly underpaid before the Outpouring. We were able to give them salary increases to make their compensation more commensurate, more *normal*. And, we were able to give bonuses for the additional hours the staff worked in the early days of the Outpouring.

Certain staff got overtime and were very blessed; some had been working 80 hours a week! They were tired, though.

As I said before, my wife and I had not had a pay raise in 13 years. The church board gave me a raise in pay, not outlandish, but at least up to an appropriate level for my responsibilities as senior pastor. My wife had worked free for three years on staff because we couldn't afford to pay her. Currently, her salary still is not commensurate with her work load. When she did get a raise it was only to match the 32 hours a week she normally worked. During the Outpouring, she worked 55 hours PLUS each week.

With the additional funds, Ignited Church caught up. There were two funds in our church that were dramatically behind: the missions fund and the benevolence fund were each $10,000 in the hole. Both of those funds have been replenished. We now have adequate resources to fund our missionaries. As a matter of fact, during the first 85 days of the Outpouring, we helped three ministries that came to us with crises, which, had it happened three months before, we would not have been able to help them with even a hundred dollars. We were able to bless each with a thousand dollars. So the additional funds have been used wisely and appropriately.

We still had to watch the budget. Carpets had to be cleaned often. Air conditioning vents and filters had to be frequently cleaned to maintain healthy air. With how fast needs came up, we had to be careful that we didn't get in trouble by going out and buying stuff on credit. So we paid cash for whatever was required.

And, the staff that I hired knew that when the Outpouring was finished, their jobs could very well be finished as well. They knew they were hired for the duration. And they were willing to take that risk. But, oh, dearest Jesus, what a ride!

Adventures of the Strader Family

Before the Outpouring the Strader family was struggling because of all the hours I had to invest in the church—being the senior pastor, taking care of all the people in the church, visiting folks in the hospital, taking phone calls, writing emails--everything it takes to pastor a church. My wife, Jan, and I had been talking: we have no family time together, no quality time. Something had to change.

It did. The Outpouring hit. Then, we had to work 70 or 80 hours a week!

The difference has been the full blossoming of spiritual growth within my family. Even now, I am astounded by it.

Before the Outpouring, Austin, my 17-year-old son, was totally into computer games. His heart's desire was to become a gaming professional. Did you know that kids can actually get paid to play video games? Austin was part of a tournament group out of Chicago. They were to fly to tournaments, get all their expenses paid, and earn $10,000 if they won. During the first six months of the Outpouring, he rarely played a game.

Austin quickly developed a passion for being in the services, for flowing in the Gifts of the Spirit. Now, when he goes to prayer meetings he often uses the Gifts of the Spirit to pray for other young people. He loves to talk about things of the spirit, and loves to be around the church.

In the first three weeks of the meetings, with services every morning and every night, we had to go to three cleaning crews. One cleaning crew would clean in the mornings as people were coming into the building, one in the afternoon to get ready for the evening, and then the thorough cleaning would happen at night, after 1:00 a.m. Austin was on the night crew (and, for the first two weeks, the morning crew as well.) He was working a lot of hours.

Austin has experienced amazing things. I'll let him tell you about one of them:

> About a week and a half into the Outpouring, we were cleaning the lobby at 3:00 a.m., and saw two teenagers sitting outside. They didn't look dangerous. So we talked to them and learned they were Southeastern students. (Southeastern is a Christian university located here in Lakeland, so we knew they were okay.) They told us, "We just wanted to be in the Presence."
>
> And we said, "So you are just sitting out front at 3:00 in the morning?"
>
> And they said, "Yeah, isn't it awesome? You can just feel the Presence."

Surprised, we said, "Oh, okay. Well, we're going back to cleaning. You guys wouldn't want to help us clean, would you?" And they thought that would be awesome.

So, as we were cleaning the bathrooms, we started praying for each other. I felt this "sheet" on my back, and so did my friend, Jeremy. We started laying hands on each other. We placed the "sheet" on one of the Southeastern kid's backs, there in the lady's bathroom. And he fell, face down on the floor, just crying.

"My back feels so weird," he said. He went off into the men's bathroom and took his shirt off. A huge scar about the size of a basketball had disappeared. It was a scar from a cancer treatment, and he got healed from the scar, and the cancer, too. God wouldn't just heal the scar, you know; he'd heal the cancer, too.

He came back and said, "Guys, the scar is gone!" We placed our hands on his back again, and we felt something moving. We actually felt it, like moving inside his back, and then it disappeared. [12]

What was amazing is that when that young man testified about his scar being healed, it led to scar after scar after scar being healed. For the next couple of weeks, just about anybody with a scar of any kind was healed.

One Lakeland woman, who had a giant hysterectomy scar across her stomach, was watching the webcast as scars were being healed, sad because she couldn't come to the meeting because of her work schedule. One morning, she drove by our church and saw the electronic sign in front. And she said, "Oh, Lord, I wish I could be in one of the meetings. I'd like for this scar to disappear." And her scar disappeared—as she drove by the church! Of course, then *her* testimony released another wave of faith, and hundreds more testified that their scars disappeared.

That's how all that happened. With my son, Austin, letting some teenagers into the church at 3:00 in the morning!

Here is another cool testimony from Austin. At the church, we had to start providing lunch for our staff. We simply could not afford the time for them to leave. So we hired a chef to cook at the church. Austin had been

---

12 Interview with Austin Strader, 6/25/2008

learning how to do Words of Knowledge. As he walked into the kitchen, his right wrist started hurting badly. He went up to the chef and asked, "Is your right wrist hurting?"

The chef—a new Christian—freaked out. "How did you know!?"

Austin said, "God just told me—and that means you're about to get healed." Austin prayed for him, and the chef was healed! Only after the healing did the chef tell him that he'd had carpal tunnel for years, with pain often to the point of tears. And it was gone!

My daughter, Alexis, wanted to go to the Outpouring every night. Twelve years old, and she had not had that much interest in things of the Spirit before the Outpouring. If we had let her she would have stayed until the last person left the tent, because she wanted to pray and be prayed over.

I hired my eldest son, Jordan, and his wife, Holly, to work on staff. Jordan is running the bookstore, and Holly became my secretary. Jordan has such business acumen that he took our bookstore from infancy to adulthood in days. He literally multiplied our bookstore sales by ten times in five days!

Janice, my wife, went from being my assistant, to stepping into a full-blown role as administrative pastor. Marvelous to watch, she literally runs the entire church. When we need to make a decision together, I sometimes hurry to make one without the full details. She just pauses, quietly, waits until I shut up, then tells me the rest of the story. I invariably come down on the side of her decision—she thinks things through so logically and carefully. Details do not fall through the cracks with Janice.

I am a most fortunate man.

Chapter Seven
How To Receive Your Miracle

In the middle of worship somebody might whack you over the head with one of those silk Jesus flags. A big foot accidentally stomped on your toe. Or maybe you got up to go to the bathroom; when you came back there was another human being sitting in your chair. Or someone saved seventy-seven seats, right in the best part of the tent, and you had to sit behind a pole. Or some jerk was standing in the middle of the crowd, messing around with the power of God, slaying others in the Spirit just for the fun of it, without the other person's permission and without an iota of respect or wisdom or reverence for God. (*You know who you are. Stop it!*) Or somebody pushed in front of you in the prayer line. Or you hated the song the worship leader was singing. Or it was too loud. Or too hot. Or too cold. Or we were having an infamous Florida thunderstorm and rain was dripping right down the back of your neck. You know—human stuff.

I always talk about the *process* of being healed or of receiving your miracle—whether it was during the Outpouring or elsewhere. There will always be the process. What it is you have to do to get to a service, what it is you have to do to get healed. You *will* have to **overcome something** in order to get your miracle or to get the hot burning coal it talks about in Isaiah 6:6.[13]

Perhaps a person may have to get over the offense of being moved down the row in order to get his miracle. It is a process, and it happens. It just happens. Are you willing to let those things go? Are you willing to display Christ's love to the person who is translating the service in Ukrainian right into the back of your ear so that you really can't hear what's being said? Are you willing to tune out the person who is in holy laughter and disturbing your deep prayer?

Are you willing not to take offense at every little thing? I'm telling you,

---

13 Then one of the seraphs flew to me with a live coal in his hand, which he had taken with tongs from the altar. With it he touched my mouth and said, "See, this has touched your lips; your guilt is taken away and your sin atoned for." Isaiah 6:6-7 (NIV)

here and now, that it will truly be difficult for God to give you a miracle when you are blocking your heart with some offense or annoyance, hatred or unforgiveness.

This is *the* most important wisdom I can impart about the process of healing. Without it, miracles can't happen for you.

Who Came for Healing, and Why

After one of our Friday morning Ministers' Seminars, I met Pastor Matthew, a priest in the Anglican Church of England. He had come across the pond with two buddies, also priests. One of his priest friends had donned a clever t-shirt with his picture on it—wearing full clerical collar and all—proclaiming, "Off Duty Priest." On the back, it said, "Got saved? Ask me how." It garnered a lot of grins and proved quite an effective evangelism technique. The three had been at the meetings for nearly a week and were going back the day we prayed together.

Serving in different parts of England, the young priests had been watching the Outpouring on God-TV from their homes. Pastor Matthew said he knew he was supposed to come to Florida the day he began a service, looked down, and realized there was only enough oil to anoint five people—with no time to get more. At the end of the service, not only had all the people been anointed, but there was more oil left than there had been at the start.

Matthew's healing at the meetings came unexpectedly. He has had a slight back condition since he was fourteen, for 25 years now. "As far as I know, I've been healed." He told his story in a low-key, matter-of-fact manner. "The way I know is that when I stand for any length of time I get this throbbing pain in my back. The last two nights I've stood for over two hours and there is no pain." Matthew went on to say that the Lord has spoken to him on a lot of different levels during his time in Florida about how He wants him to increase prayer for the sick. No doubt Matthew's prayers will be multiplied in power simply because of his own *experience* of physical healing. He will be a true witness.

To many, the image of the Church of England is of a staid religious group to whom the Outpouring would seem a remote thing. Matthew told us, however, that the church is quite diverse, with a Charismatic stream running within it. As priests, they are well educated theologically, but are not skilled in healings and miracles. "You have to get trained by coming to conferences like this," he admitted. "We are going back to tell the Anglican Church what we have experienced."

Other people came, flat out *expecting* their healing. Perhaps they had been healed before, or seen others healed. Or were accustomed to worshipping in a church where healings are considered *normal*. At any rate, these people were more comfortable with the whole idea.

Back in October, 2006, Minnesotan Robert T. suffered a devastating stroke, followed by fifteen mini strokes during the ensuing week. Robert and his wife Judy learned that one of the carotid arteries in the back of his neck had never worked since birth, and the other artery now had a 90% blockage.

The neurologist told them, "Well, we can either wait for the big one or we can send you to the Mayo Clinic." Robert and Judy packed their bags and went to Rochester. The stint in his neck failed, and the doctors came back to the room, puzzled. "We don't know what is keeping Robert alive." They had taken an angiogram and found that the artery was indeed blocked, so Robert *should* have been dead.

They sent Robert for yet another MRI. The doctors found that the Lord had taken the vein that was coming from the front and re-routed it to the back of his head. I don't know what that means medically, but the astounded doctors proclaimed it a miracle. Something like that could have happened over a long period of time, they said, but not instantly like this! Doctors compared Robert's three prior MRI's to this new one and realized: God had performed a miracle, indeed.

However, Robert was told that he would never see, and probably never walk again. Now he walks, and has recovered a limited tunnel vision. He actually sees color, which the doctors also said would never happen. Robert and Judy came to the Outpouring, expecting God to complete his miracle so that he can see completely again.

The night before, they had gone up on stage and been prayed for. Their daughter back home, who is blessed with frequent visions and dreams, heard the Lord say, "Turn the television on. Your Mom and Dad are going to be healed." The service was just going off the air. So she raced to the computer and pulled up the website. Just as it came up, her Dad was on the stage, with Todd ready to pray over him!

Later, the Lord gave her a vision. The healing that was to come for her Dad was not as they had specified in their prayers, but it would be coming. All of a sudden, she saw bright lights shooting out of her Mom and Dad. In the next part of the dream, she saw her Dad, running in white tennis shoes. He hadn't been able to do that since the stroke. Judy said, "It was another confirmation. We are just giving the Lord praise. We love to tell the story to anyone who will listen." They are strong in their faith that Robert's healing is coming—as *they go*. There was no doubt in their minds.

...As They Went

Some critics lambasted the Outpouring, pointing out that not every one was healed on stage. They made the assumption that the only kind of healing is instantaneous. And that's not true. Many people are healed, *as they go*.

Jesus healed the lepers, and they were healed "as they went." Only one leper actually came back and testified (and gave Jesus thanks.) And he was the one who was actually made whole. The others were cleansed of their leprosy, but they still had missing fingers and toes. But the one who came back got his toes and fingers restored. He came back with a grateful heart, and I conjecture that brought the fullness of his healing.[14]

The speaker frequently says, "Some people will be instantly healed. Some people will be touched tonight, and your healing will begin. For others, your healing will come when God releases it." There are many examples of people who were healed the third or fourth night they were there.

Some in the tent didn't even believe in miracles. In fact, some of them wouldn't have been caught dead in a healing service. Until they got a doctor's death sentence on their heads. Then they didn't care. They wanted a miracle. They wanted to live. Out of desperation, they came to the wildest Pentecostal meeting on the planet Earth to get a miracle.

---

14 As Jesus continued on toward Jerusalem, he reached the border between Galilee and Samaria. As he entered a village there, ten lepers stood at a distance, crying out, "Jesus, Master, have mercy on us!" He looked at them and said, "Go show yourselves to the priests." And as they went, they were cleansed of their leprosy. One of them, when he saw that he was healed, came back to Jesus, shouting, "Praise God!" He fell to the ground at Jesus' feet, thanking him for what he had done. This man was a Samaritan. Jesus asked, "Didn't I heal ten men? Where are the other nine? Has no one returned to give glory to God except this foreigner?" And Jesus said to the man, "Stand up and go. . Your faith has healed you."
Luke 17: 11-19 (NIV)

And, because they saw other people experiencing miracles, they set aside their predisposition that this was impossible, out of the hope and the desperation that maybe, just maybe, they could also get a miracle. Faith is the substance of things that are "hoped" for. They came into the room and they felt it. "My God, this is really real! I could be healed tonight!"

At that moment, when faith dropped in their heart and the speaker said, "I feel God is touching hearts right now. If you have heart trouble, get up here now!" They didn't even think about it. They leapt out of their seat and ran to the front, and the moment hands were laid on them, they were healed. All because the proverbial angel stirred the pool of Bethesda waters and they jumped in. And they were healed. And that is how the miracles often happened, in the tent.

Now, here's the problem. Whenever somebody is healed because of somebody else's faith, they are at a high risk to lose their healing. The Bible says, *"Whenever Satan is cast out of a body, he goes out into dry places. Then he goes back to the house he used to live in. If he finds it swept and garnished, he brings seven other devils with him."*[15] So if you were healed by somebody else's faith, then you have to fill up your own life with faith. Then, when Satan comes back, he will be met with the power of the Holy Spirit. You will resist the devil and he will flee from you, and you won't lose your healing.[16]

Not Only Physical Healings

Sometimes we get focused thinking that only physical healings came from the meetings. That is far from the truth. One of Father Matthew's Anglican priest friends went through a great crisis during his visit to Florida, followed by a great healing. There were emotional healings, spiritual ones, healings of forgiveness…whatever was required.

One of my best friends from Bible School days has throat cancer. He's not much for healing meetings, but he is one of those with a death sentence over his head. So he came to Lakeland, like so many others.
He is a renaissance man. He's an inventor and has designed church buildings. He was the road manager for a well-respected Christian musician. Once, he even designed and built a natural waterfall for Billy Graham's home in Asheville, NC—as a gift. And he has a tremendous

---

15 Luke 11:24-26 KJV
16 We offer a little booklet, "How to Keep Your Healing," by Kenneth Hagin. He gives substantive information about healings. I recommend it—highly.

will to live.

When he came to Lakeland he was very weak. But he went to the evening meeting at the tent—that long, loud, rowdy meeting. I can't imagine what he thought! But leaving after the meeting, he saw me and my family crossing the road, directly in front of his car! (Just God being God, don't you know?) We stopped and prayed for him, then and there.

The next morning, he went to a church building he had designed in a nearby city, and which he had not seen since its completion. He went up to the altar and just looked around, quietly. Suddenly, the pastor came out and, upon learning who my friend was, prayed for him, right there.

Later, my old friend and his wife went for a ride together. Passing one front yard, they saw a man out mowing his lawn and came screeching to a halt. It was the pastor who had officiated their wedding! They chatted and, before they left, the pastor prayed for them, as well.

They drove to Starbucks for their caffeine fix. While they were inside the shop, Todd Bentley walked in! Now, you have to understand, Todd was never able to go into Starbucks in Lakeland! He couldn't. He would get mobbed. He had to send in one of his associates. But today, this one day, Todd Bentley walked into Starbucks. And my friend worked up enough courage to ask him for prayer. Todd prayed. Right in the middle of Starbucks!

Later that day, my friend came to my office. He told me all about his day's astounding adventures. When I asked if he was going back to the evening meeting, he gave me a slow, gentle smile. "No," he said, "I think I got what I came for. I am filled." And with that, my friend went home. I don't know what kind of healing he received, but it was quite apparent that he was at peace.

Healing from a Suicidal Spirit

If you watched on television or the internet, or if you came to the meetings, you may have seen a big, handsome man sitting off to the left side of the platform. He was keeping watch to be sure that nobody was harmed. His name is Eduardo Juarez. His miracles, and how he came to be sitting on that stage, will stagger your mind.

I live about three hours from Lakeland, so getting to the Outpouring is kind of an ordeal. I came to the first meeting because my second youngest daughter is hearing-impaired. I brought her, along with my oldest daughter, simply with the intention for her to receive a physical healing. I had no idea what the Outpouring had in store for *me*.

About 45 days prior to that meeting, my wife had asked me for a divorce. I was a great provider and protector, but I was a horrible husband. I had abused her emotionally. Prior to and during our marriage I had multiple affairs—not only sexual infidelity, but emotional relationships, what I thought of as "soul" ties. I would be home for several months, then I'd move out and live with another woman. I was still providing income for my wife and children, but I was also involved in drugs, heavy drinking, and several motorcycle clubs. I was never abusive to my wife physically, but you can imagine all the emotional scars. As my children got older, they got to see me going in and out of the home. Scar on top of scar on top of scar.

In 2002, while I was living with yet another woman, I heard the very still Voice of God, and I came to Him. That very night, God began to close the door on that unfaithful relationship. I knew in the natural it was time for me to go home. But God didn't want me to go home the same way I had in the past. So I gave my life to God. And I went home that night. Astonishingly, my wife received me and forgave me.

Some time later, as I was cleaning up my motorcycle, she told me that she and the girls were going to church. I said, "Wait for me. I want to go, too." In that moment, a holy hush came into the house.

My daughters had been saved at Vacation Bible School two years prior to that, and they had been praying for their Mom to be saved. A year or so later, my wife gave her life to the Lord. My two children and my wife—plus a core group of five other women— had been interceding for me to come back to God.

I had grown up in the church. A wonderful black pastor and his wife adopted my mother and her five children, and took us under their wing. As time went on our bond grew with the pastor and his wife—and it also grew with the body of his church.

At some point, my family and I assumed responsibility as caretakers of the church. I began to cut the lawn, clean the windows and front door. I shoveled snow in the winter. On Saturday afternoons we vacuumed and mopped the floors, got on our knees and scrubbed the toilets, made things spic and span for church on Sunday.

I was my Dad's personal aide in the church—I'd carry his Bible and did whatever he needed. I got to see the inner workings of the church and hear great men of God. God allowed me, at such a young age, to become a servant of the church. In my experiences now I am beginning to see that even back then I had become a servant of the tabernacle.

I wouldn't be here today had it not been for my mother raising me in the church. Raise up your child in the way he should go, and when he is old, he will not depart from it. When he is old… That doesn't say anything about what might happen in the interim.

I chose to walk away.

Now, I must tell you something very painful. I was sexually abused as a young boy. I was physically and emotionally abused, inside the church and out. I hurry to say that it was *NOT* that wonderful pastor. And he did *not* know what was happening.

But in my child's mind, I could not figure out why he didn't know, and stop it. And I could not understand why God didn't know, and stop it. How could you allow me to be hurt, if I was growing up in the church? Why would you allow me to be hurt? My spirit was crying out, raging, why doesn't any one know that this is happening to me? During these times of abuse, I would literally cry out to God, why are You letting this happen to me? It planted seeds of rebellion in me. And I walked away from the church.

My mother never lost faith in me. She told me before I left for the Marine Corps that I would never make a good sinner, because I knew God. But do you know what I *heard*? I heard that I wouldn't be any good. Period.

So when I left for the Marine Corps, I started living a life of excess. If a buddy was drinking one can of beer, I'd try to drink a case. If he was drinking a shot of whiskey, I'd try to drink the bottle. If you were doing one line of cocaine, I would do triple. And I said to myself, "No one will ever abuse me again. If I am going to be abused again, it will be because I choose to abuse myself."

Every person at some time in their life is a victim. At some point you become the abuser. The way you manifest the abuse may not be the way you were abused, but nonetheless you become an abuser.

What I saw in women was what I saw in myself—my weakness as a young boy, being unable to protect myself. And I didn't like it. I would get mad. So I would emotionally abuse women. I would captivate them just to see how many I could get. I was remembering how weak I was as a young boy. *Hurting me because of my weakness...* So I became a controller and manipulator of women. I was a liar, a cheater, abuser, victim, adulterer. It followed me even after I met my wife. I began to have affairs on top of affairs.

But the whole time I was one of those people the evangelists talk about who watch Christian television late at night. I knew God. I wanted God. But I was mad at God. But, in 2002, on that blessed night when I gave my life to God, I prayed, "In the world I live my life in excess. I want to serve You in excess. So this is my simple prayer to you, God: I come to You and I will serve You. But don't make me one of those Christians who sit in the back pew, because if that is what You are going to do, I'd rather die." My repentance prayer was: For God I live; for God I die....

I was giving God authority to bring all my ugliness and put it in front of my face. So from 2002 until the Outpouring, I had been *trying* to walk with God. But as many successes as I had in God, I had that many failures in God. In my public life I was success. But in my private life, I was a fiasco—a hypocrite.

I've worked in homeless ministries, counseled young boys in trouble and men in prison. My wife and I have even helped counsel troubled marriages, if you can believe that. When I came to God that night in 2002 when I went to church with my wife, the miraculous thing God did was to let me begin to understand how much He loves me. It's been a work in progress even to this moment. But I'm starting to understand God's grace. Grace! Even in my failures and in my flesh, He still loves me! That is the reason, even more so now, that I passionately love God. I desperately want every man to know that it is okay for God to love you. To allow God to flood you with His love. And to know His Grace.

After hearing that my wife wanted a divorce, I was wrecked emotionally. I began to fall into old mindsets of my former life. I was so stunned by the fact that she wanted a divorce that I went looking for any feeling at all because I was simply numb.

Numb. From the time my wife asked me for a divorce to the night in Tiger Stadium, I literally worked six days a week, sometimes for 14 hours. One day I worked 20 hours. I was so busy, all I had strength to do was drive home and pass out. Numb. We weren't sleeping in the same bed; I had moved into the garage. We were already preparing separate bank accounts. Preparing divorce papers. Looking for a place for me to move into. She wanted me out.

By profession I am a surgical scrub tech. I have even gone to Africa and Honduras on surgical mission trips. So, in my medical knowledge I know that with healing in the natural, often there are underlying issues with emotional problems.

That's what kept drawing me to the healing Outpouring. I knew there was something more for me than healing in the natural sense. What I was experiencing was that my heart was broken. This is where interaction with the Outpouring began. "So we'll try this one more time, God. We'll do this dance one more time. I'll give You my heart, but don't hurt me again."

What I was referring to was how my heart was hurt physically and emotionally when I was a young boy. When I came to God in 2002, I repented and I thoroughly changed my life. I thought that not only had my life and heart been restored, I sincerely believed that God had restored my wife's heart, as well. I did not realize that she had to receive God's healing for herself. Because of my countless years of abuse, she never let God get into her heart. So when we began to have marital problems and my old stuff came back on me, she began to suffer the old hurts that she felt before I came to God. Not wanting those hurts again, she said, "I want a divorce."

From the outside, our marriage looked like a success. Walking in the Word together, doing this and that together, we were a public success. People could point us out and say, "See? God *can* restore a husband to his wife." What they didn't know is that some people may be a public success, but in their private lives are failures. And that's what my wife and I were.

So I told God, "You hurt me. You let me get hurt again. How could you heal my heart and not heal my wife's heart?" I didn't realize that my wife had to willingly let God heal her heart.

I decided to commit suicide. I had a gun. I kept it loaded. And I kept it on me. I told God: when I am by myself, I am going to do it. I didn't want to hurt my wife or kids or anybody else. I just wanted to do what I couldn't do as a child. *I wanted to stop the pain.*

It was the first night at Tiger Stadium and it was a Saturday night. And my wife and daughters had decided to come, too. Todd began to give Words of Knowledge. "Someone here is being tormented." I can't be for sure what he said exactly, but what I heard was: somebody here is being tormented by a suicidal spirit. And that was me.

He kept saying, "Somebody here, somebody here..." And I remember saying, "Don't mess with me right now, God." But Todd just kept on and on. It was like having an argument with God. Stop it. I'm not giving You another chance.

I had the gun on me that night. I had all intentions to commit suicide, off by myself someplace. But God kept on and on, and wouldn't let me go.

So I said to myself, "If you're going to do it, better do it now." So

I told God, "Okay, I surrender."

Have you ever seen the statue of the man holding the world on his shoulders? That's what I felt like. I was carrying everybody's world that I had taken responsibility for. When I said, "I surrender," that weight lifted off! I physically felt it. No longer hunched over, burdened down. I just felt light. God took off the weight of the world that I had put on myself! God had been there all the time and I hadn't realized it!

I wanted to tell Todd that it was me he was talking about. But my wife and kids were there. How could I shame them? But I found an intern, and I told him. "Listen, that guy Todd was talking about? That's me."

He did the Christian thing. "Are you okay? Do you want me to pray for you?"

"No, you don't understand. That's ME! That's ME!" I hadn't captured his attention like I felt like I needed to. I said, "Look in the bag." When he saw the gun he knew it was true.

I thank God for that young man, because I fed off his courage. I told him, "Listen, just do me a favor. I'm not going up there. I don't want to freak people out. I don't want to get taken down as a nut. I'm going to take the gun now and go put it in my car." I asked, "Just tell Todd that you met the gentleman he was talking about."

I thought that would be the end of it. Well, at some point that young man told Todd, and Todd told him to find me. He must have thought, "Impossible. How am I gonna find that guy in all these people?"

After the meeting, my wife and kids went home. But I went back to Tiger Stadium the next night. And would you believe it, God let that young man locate me!

He was so excited. "I told Todd about you, and he is excited! He's been thinking about you all day, and he wants to meet you." Cool, I thought. I'm going to get a meet-and-greet and some personal prayer from Todd. So I told the young man where I was seated.

Twenty minutes later he came back. "Todd wants to talk to you. They're already out on the stage." I thought Todd would just walk down the steps in the back, bless me and pray over me, and that would be it.

He walked me down to the field. I remember the young man having to tell all the interns, "He's with me. He's okay." At the time, I weighed 265 lbs., had long hair, a tank top and big tattoos. So I can understand his saying, "He's okay, he's with me."

I'm following behind like a puppy. I'm going to meet a great man of God... He walked me behind the stage near the Fresh Fire associates. They're staring, obviously wondering what's up. I don't look like a very wholesome Christian.

I have always longed to be truly loved and accepted by the Body of God. But I never really have felt that. I always stood out. The pastor and wife who adopted us were a black family. We went to an all black church. Even the people of my own race—Mexican-American—didn't accept me because I was the black pastor's son, living in the black community.

So, while I was waiting, Evangelist Jim Drown[17] came over and told me about his life—so similar to my own. The fact that he had discernment that I wasn't what I looked like meant everything to me. When he told the other associates that I was okay, it could have stopped there and been okay. Someone valued me enough to defend me. To some it may seem a little thing—that someone saw value in me—but to me, it was everything.

The next person who came to me was evangelist Kira Mitchell, who was doing interviews before someone went up onto the platform. She said, "I just want to get some facts." I still did not have a clue. Then she says, "You're going to be the first person to speak to him. So when you get up there..."

What! Get up where? Up on the platform? Huh-uh. No. Nope. Are you out of your mind? I don't want my wife and kids and

---

17 Jim Drown, of Global Evangelistic Missions.

family to know what I had been planning to do. Kira calmly said, "Eduardo, do you realize how powerful this testimony is? How many people are going to hear you? In 214 countries?"

She was actually giving me reasons *not* to do it.

Then, I heard Kira tell me this: Christians don't believe that other Christians battle with suicide. They think they are the only one. No Christian would admit thoughts of suicide.

I said OK. Then I thought, "Oh, God, I really didn't say that, did I?"

We went up on stage. I felt like every eyeball in the stadium was on me. They were going to call the cops on me. Put me in the hospital…

As I was waiting to be ministered to, Todd was talking to the crowd. Have you ever been too close to a firecracker when it went off? I couldn't hear what Todd was saying. When they talk about the weightiness and Glory of God being in and around the stage and altar area, it is real. I was in shock. I was in the Glory of God.

I heard Todd say, "Kira, who do you have here?" She began to tell my testimony. Todd was trying to coax me into telling my story. It wasn't working. I simply could not talk.

I don't remember anything after that until I was at the bottom of the stage. People were coming up and blessing me and saying, "We honor you for giving your testimony." As I walked away, I suddenly realized I hadn't shared my testimony with my wife. Was she watching on God-TV? Over 200 countries—oh, God. I had to call my wife, right now, and explain.

I found a quiet corner and called my wife. "Uh, honey, you know that thing we have where you've got to tell each other before it comes out?" Yes. "Um, well…." And she said, "What did you do now?"

Stop. Stop. Stop. I must tell you something else. This is

God, being God! The prior Saturday my wife had gone to an Outpouring meeting at the Life Church in Auburndale. Todd gave a word of knowledge that there was a woman who needed a heart transplant. My wife said she knew that he was talking about her. But she didn't go up to the platform, because another woman who *physically* needed a heart transplant had gone up to receive that word of knowledge.

My wife was being sensitive. Up until that point it had been a healing outpouring — the physical aspects, not emotional. But, get this. She physically saw the hand of God reach into her heart, take out her old heart, and put a new one in. *I'm going to give you a new heart for your husband.*

In one week's time, God had healed me, healed her, and completely restored our marriage and our family.

I had to repay God in some way. On my off days, I started carrying a Bible. I was going back and forth to the meetings — three hours away. Just prior to my healing at Tiger Stadium, I had a job. You can imagine all the pressure. I had to take some personal time off. I did *not* lie and say I was sick. When I returned to work on my scheduled day, I was told that I was being put on suspension. I had missed too many days going to the Outpouring. Less than a week later, I was terminated.

I wasn't mad. And I really wasn't confused. At some point along the way, God had made my wife and me be at peace with everything that was going to happen. I didn't know what that meant. Even now, I still don't know what all that means.

But, after weeks of volunteering as an aide, usher, trash collector, catcher, and whatever else needed to be done, I was honored to be asked to be on the Lakeland staff of Fresh Fire Ministries.

Daily, I get to hear great men and women of God, see people miraculously healed, feel the compassion and desperation of people coming to hear God and feel God. To just soak in these people's anointing. And, for Fresh Fire to think that I'm not some whack job and allow me to be part of this…it is humbling.[18]

18 Interview with Eduardo Juarez, 7/25/2008.

Eduardo is now on staff at Ignited Church, helping us with security. It is a blessing to have him here.

Chapter Eight
A Doctor's Voice: Is It Real?

Does God heal? Are miracles verifiable? Yes, on both counts. However, the vast majority of miracles are self-reported. Pain left. Can hear better. Stomach pain is gone. I can now walk after being in a wheel chair for years. Many of the reports of healing are true and are wonderful stories, but are not medically documented.

People do not come to meetings with medical records, and getting follow-up tests of specific healings often requires a long turnaround time and even major expense. Many healthcare providers are unwilling to attribute any change of a patient's condition to the result of prayer and divine intervention. So, the number who have time to go back to their healthcare professionals and go through the expense and the hassle of getting insurance approval for follow-up MRI's, EKG's, and other tests would be small. But even if a small handful of miracles were medically verifiable, that is important. We do have a number of healings with good, verifiable reports.

Fresh Fire and Ignited Church have received medical documentation on several healings and have asked a currently licensed and board certified physician to review the files and give his opinion regarding whether or not the medical evidence supports the claims of healing. His review of the information submitted for certain patients justifies the claim, he says, that there have been medically verifiable healings.

The doctor shared three examples of verifiable healings. There was a case of a woman with severe scoliosis who was certain she was going to be healed, so before she went to the Outpouring, she had a person take a picture of her bare back from the waist up. That photograph shows severe curvature of the spine. The woman went to the Outpouring that night and was healed. The next day, she had another photograph taken in the same pose showing the spine very straight. This is an instance where the healing is verified by photographs which have been reviewed by a doctor.

Doctors found a lesion about the size of a half dollar in another person's liver. Immediately, the doctors scheduled a follow-up MRI to be done the next day. That evening, however, the patient and family came for prayer at the Outpouring. After prayer, the patient believed healing had occurred, and the MRI taken the following day confirmed it. It showed no lesion. It was a medically verified miracle.

Perhaps one of the more dramatic healings occurred in a person with severe kidney failure. The head of the nephrology department of a well-known university medical center wrote a letter (on university letterhead), stating that the patient was in poor health, with her renal function deteriorating rapidly. The woman's kidneys were functioning at only a 25% level. After prayer, the woman's renal function was again evaluated and found to have improved to 75 to 80% normal function. The only answer, the doctor wrote, is that, "This God of yours healed you. "

As an example of how difficult it is at times to obtain medical verification, the university center requested the head of nephrology not to use university letterhead when reporting this story! The university did not want its named used in the reporting of this healing. Many don't want to get in the middle of the divine healing controversy.

The physician reviewing the stories of healing for Fresh Fire and Ignited Church strongly advised neither to give out the names and addresses of the individuals healed nor to share names of healthcare professionals or institutions. HIPPA regulations prohibit health care institutions from sharing private medical information. Even if a person gives permission to share information, it is not the responsibility of Fresh Fire or Ignited Church to share this personal information with the media. Instead, it is far wiser to have qualified healthcare professionals review any medical documentation and then verify the findings, as was being done in these instances.

Would *you* want TV cameras and newspaper and magazine reporters crammed around your door, demanding an interview? Some people could handle the publicity, but a lot could not. It would crush them. As noted above, many healthcare institutions don't want the media pressures either. What Fresh Fire and Ignited Church tried to do was to create a format where the media could be provided reliable information without exposing the people to an onslaught from the media.

Resurrections and Near Death Experiences

After the doctor's careful review of several reports of resurrections, it became clear that several of the claimed resurrections were indeed miraculous—but should more correctly be medically classified as "miraculous instances of resuscitation."

One such story involved a child that was found in a pond, face down, for fifteen to twenty minutes. Attempts to resuscitate him failed. But then, following much prayer, he revived, with no neurological damage. "I have seen a number of near death experiences like that. If a child is in water that is cold enough, they can come back." But this water was warm from the summer sun! Whether it was resuscitation or resurrection does not lessen the wonderful blessing of the Lord bringing the child back to life!

There is, however, a report from Guatemala of a child being resurrected that appears, from the information submitted to Fresh Fire and Ignited Church, to be a true, verifiable instance of being raised from the dead. Resurrections have been reported around the world by a number of evangelists, missionaries and pastors in recent church history. To those that believe, no proof is necessary. To those that don't believe, no proof is possible.

The Boy Found in the Pond

Theresa[19] had been watching the Outpouring on God TV for many weeks. She was at a ball field watching a game when her cell phone rang. Here is her story.

> My grandson Korvan was 14 months old. It was the middle of June in Tennessee. It was quite warm out at that time of year. My daughter Christy and son-in-law Troy noticed little Korvan was not in the kitchen with their other two sons, Zion and Silas. They were 3 and 5 years old. Troy noticed the back door was slightly open. He ran outside around the house to find Korvan floating in a landscape pool they had for frogs for the boys.
>
> Christy heard a blood curdling scream from Troy as she had never heard before! She ran outside to find Troy holding Korvan in his arms ever so limp! She said he looked like a corpse! He was not

19 Last name withheld to protect the family from any unnecessary press. The family has been interviewed multiple times and we believe their story to be credible.

breathing and had no heartbeat! Christy said she needed to go back into the kitchen to be able to pray in faith. She couldn't bear to look at him that way!

I was at the soccer fields with my youngest daughter, 11 year old Jessica, when I received a call on my cell phone. This is what I heard. "Mom, Korvan is dead, pray that he comes back to life!" I immediately hung up the phone. My other son-in-law Charles was also at the fields with his daughter named Faith. I grabbed his arm and told him the call I had just received from Christy. We both went into prayer immediately!

In the meantime, Troy and a Christian brother of his were also at the house at the time of the drowning. His friend Ben knew a little CPR which he performed on Korvan. There was still no sign of life! Korvan was not breathing for at least 20 minutes. They are not sure how long he was in the water before they found him. His skin was cold! Finally, Troy spoke over Korvan, "I command life to come back into your body in the Name of Jesus!"

Just then Korvan coughed, and his eyes were rolled back into his head! He started to take his first breath! He was still very limp! I then received another call from Christy to tell me he was breathing, and to keep on praying. I am a nurse. She asked me what she should do next. His body is so cold and limp! I told her to take him in the house and warm him in blankets. By the end of the evening Korvan jumped off Christy's lap and wanted to eat some banana bread!

During the night hours Korvan developed a high fever! His lungs had been filled with water. Christy called her father and me to tell us about his high fever. It was about 6 AM. I told her if the Lord Jesus Christ brought him back to life, He would surely do a complete work of healing his body!

When Korvan woke up, his fever was totally gone! And, he had been born severely bowlegged. But now his legs were almost straight! We sure serve an awesome God!

After a few days went by Christy and Troy told us more testimonies of other friends who had been alerted of Korvan's drowning. They were also praying for him. One couple was praying together when the Lord directed them to read about the resurrection power of Christ and pray about it. It was only minutes later they received a call from Christy telling them to pray for Korvan to be raised from the dead!

This was a summer I will never forget as long as I live! I shared this with all my coworkers. It brought tears to even the non-believers. I know it touched their hearts and caused them to think twice about our great wonderful Father in heaven!

Christy and Troy are preparing to do some missions work in Mexico. A lot of hard work is ahead of them. Keep them in your prayers as they trust the Father to provide all that is needed for this endeavor. They plan on being there for quite some time.

Chapter Nine
Healed As They Came—And Went!

Jesus sowed his seed in our hearts, then off he went....
He knew things would not be ideal.

There were the birds and the droughts,
the weeds and the insects,
the parasites and the blights.

But there was also the power of the seed itself.

--Joseph G. Donders[20]

The great California pastor, Bill Johnson, says, "When God brings revelation to his people, he does not do it to make them smarter." The purpose of revelation is to lead us in a revolution—to revolutionize our thinking in what we can expect from the King.

It is not good enough simply to *believe* in divine healing. We can believe, yet never experience it for ourselves. You can *believe* that Christ has given you the power to release healing and activate healing in others, yet never know the thrill of having Christ's power flow through your hands as you raise a dead man from his deathbed, or watch a crooked limb grow straight, or see sight restored or a deaf ear opened. Believe it can happen? Yes. But it never happens for you. Why not?

Jesus said, "You will receive *power* when the Holy Spirit comes on you."[21] Have you ever received the Power of God? The power. The *dunamis*. As I've said before, d*unamis* is a Greek word that means power, strength, authority, enablement, empowerment. It is the root word for "dynamite." Let me ask you a question. Where is the power, the *dunamis*?

---

20 Joseph G. Donders, teacher and chaplain, University of Nairobi, Kenya.
21 "But the Holy Spirit will come upon you and give you power. Then you will tell everyone about me in Jerusalem, in all Judea, in Samaria, and everywhere in the world." Acts 1:8

We think the baptism of the Holy Spirit is a "Rondai, shondai, she rode off on the Hyundai." It never says in the Bible that when you receive the Holy Spirit you will speak in tongues. That just happens to be *evidence*. It *does* say that when you encounter the Holy Spirit you are supposed to have *power*.

And not just power, but power and authority. To tread upon all the things of the enemy, and nothing shall hurt you.[22] You become the Terminator. Absolutely nothing will stop you. Your mission is impossible in the eyes of humanity. But all things are possible in the eyes of God.

Jesus said that when the Holy Spirit comes upon you, you will become a witness. Take a look. That is the last part of that scripture verse:

"But the Holy Spirit will come upon you and give you power. Then you will tell everyone about me in Jerusalem, in all Judea, in Samaria, and everywhere in the world."

You become a witness. Not just a third party. Not just an echo. But a *voice*.

If an accident takes place out on highway 98, and you come upon it, a policeman might come over to you and ask, "Sir, tell me what happened."

And you say, "Well, it appears to me that this car was going this way and the other car came in and hit it."

And the policeman says, "Oh, so you didn't actually see the accident."

You admit, "No, sir. I didn't."

And the policeman turns around and goes to find somebody who actually saw what happened. He has to have an actual eyewitness.

God wants *YOU* to be an actual eyewitness, to be able to send out your own email report. We've just been telling Bible stories. We've been telling stories that we read on the internet, or from books, or from sermons that we heard. But we weren't there. We didn't have the *experience*.

---

22 Luke 10:19

Let's examine Jesus' *experience*:

On a Sabbath Jesus was teaching in one of the synagogues, and a woman was there who had been crippled by a spirit for eighteen years. She was bent over and could not straighten up at all. When Jesus saw her, he called her forward and said to her, "Woman, you are set free from your infirmity."

Woman, thou art loosed!

Then he put his hands on her, and immediately she straightened up and praised God.

Indignant because Jesus had healed on the Sabbath, the synagogue ruler said to the people, "There are six days for work. So come and be healed on those days, not on the Sabbath."

The Lord answered him, "You hypocrites! Doesn't each of you on the Sabbath untie his ox or donkey from the stall and lead it out to give it water? Then should not this woman, a daughter of Abraham, whom Satan has kept bound for eighteen long years, be set free on the Sabbath day from what bound her?"

When he said this, all his opponents were humiliated, but the people were delighted with all the wonderful things he was doing.[23]

Sabbath day was a holy day, a church day, a synagogue day…the place for the Word to be preached. A place to have prayers. But not, apparently, a place to be healed, or to have demons cast out, or to be set free from bondage.

Theologians insist that you can't cast demons out of Christians. Tell that to the Christian who is bound by the demon. Tell that to the demon. I am not going to argue with you whether the demon is inside or outside or attached or floating around in the atmosphere. Just get rid of the foul thing.

Perhaps you are a spirit-filled believer, speaking in tongues more than anyone else in your church. Yet you are struggling with pornography. Can't control your temper. Have one sickness after another after another.

---

23 Luke 13:10-17 (NIV).

Can't hold your marriage together. Kids are in rebellion. And they say a Christian can't have a demon? Bondage is something that has you bound. A stronghold is something that has a strong hold on you. Get rid of it.

Have you ever noticed that the theologians never cast out demons or release people from bondage? "If you want to tell me how to prophesy, sir, show me. Demonstrate. If you want to show me how to cast out devils, show me. Do it. And when you start casting out more demons than I, then I will listen to you. When you start getting more people out of wheelchairs than I, then I will listen to you."

Please, good people, don't separate my words from my heart. I am not being arrogant. I am trying to teach you that what happened in this Outpouring is beyond our theological boxes. It was beyond our church growth principles. It was outside the lines. As Bishop Clarice Fluitt says, "God gives you an *experience*. Then God gives you an *explanation*." We were getting the experience.

About two weeks into the Outpouring, I was sitting on the platform, writing reports on my laptop. (Did you receive the email reports about the meetings? Well, that was me. I sat there writing down what was happening.) Suddenly, Todd said, "Wait a minute. He's just come into the room. The angel has just come into the room."

And I was typing, "Wait a minute. He's just come into the room. The angel has just come into the room…"

As I hit the enter key, I felt what I later perceived to be a wing of the angel hit me in my chair, front on, from my toes to the top of my head. The wing went through my body, in the front and out the back. It hit me so hard that I grabbed my laptop and went backwards in my chair. Bishop Clarice Fluitt was sitting beside me, and she grabbed me by my shirt to keep me from falling. The electrical current of God went up her arm and knocked her over to the left, and she almost went out of her chair. All of that happened in about three seconds or less. I—*we*—just had an experience of God. Ever since then, I have been very, very sensitive to the Holy Spirit, greater than I ever have before.

The next morning when I woke up, I loved my wife more, I loved my kids more, I loved Jesus more, I even loved the dog more that peed on the carpet and really irritated me. I loved everything more. So I'm thinking, "This experience equals loving God more. This experience must be good."

I won't get the explanation of *what* happened that night—and *why*—until later. Perhaps much later. But I will get it. I am confident of that. Right now, I don't care. I had an experience of God. And it has made me love Jesus even more.

What I am trying to tell you is that there are things we don't understand. Like people talking about angels. And portals. What's that all about? *I don't know.*

I do know, however, about our doctrine. Our doctrine has to be straight, unmistakable, unblemished. We made sure people know that Jesus Christ is King of Kings and Lord of Lords. He is the one true God. He was born of a virgin. He died. He rose from the dead. He ascended into the heaven. And He is now seated at the right hand of the Father.

The Fine Print of God

In the sovereignty of God, there are people who, for whatever reason, in the mind and scope of God, won't receive their healing in this life. This is the fine print of God. I don't know why that should be. You won't hear the Word of Faith preacher give this to you, but I will. You need to know it.

There were times in Jesus' life when he stepped past people, and only healed the one. Jesus ministered to the Roman centurion's daughter who died—why not a nice Jewish girl? There were thousands pressing around Jesus that day, but the woman with the issue of blood, "unclean," was the one who got her healing. Even in the Old Testament, the prophet was sent to a widow woman who wasn't even a Jew. She was a gentile, a heathen. And, Rahab—the harlot—was the only one to survive the destruction of Jericho. There are things about God's sovereignty that I cannot explain.

I am, however, obligated to tell you what I *do* know. And what I know is this: The Word says, "By His stripes we were healed." *By. His. Stripes. We. Were. Healed.*

My job was—and is—to build your faith. If you were a group of Olympic champions, and all I did was to show you the people who failed—those people who missed it by hundredths of a point, or the people who had seemingly wasted eight years of their lives getting up at five o'clock in the morning to train for their one moment, then pulled a hamstring and couldn't compete—what kind of a coach would I be?

And, if all I showed you were the people who didn't get healed—the people who flew here and spent their last dollar and didn't get their healing and went home and died—it would not produce faith.

That's why I tell you about the ones who *did* get their healing. The woman who *did* rise. The man who *did* get his eyesight restored. The little child whose ears *were* opened. I show you the faith-builders. That does not make me a deceiver.

I do not have all the answers. But I *do* know that if somebody is bound, it is *not* right! My job is to set people free.

My Jesus said, *it is not right that this daughter of Abraham be bound for eighteen years.* I don't care if it is the Sabbath day, she's getting healed.

It is not right that you suffer with your diabetes, and your heart problems, and your family situation. It's not right that you have all of these problems with your finances and your relationships. It's not right that you struggle from hand to mouth day after day. It's not right for you to be bound in Egypt. It's not right for you to wander in the wilderness.

What *is* right is that He's taking you to a promise land, flowing with milk and honey. He just doesn't bother to tell you that there are giants in the land, and you are going to have to kill some to get the honey. There is something big that you are going to have to overcome, remember?

When you showed up, you discovered the giants. "Well, y'know, it's too hot to stand in line... I have had diabetes for a long time... I can't stand the sound in the room... It's so loud... Why do they play the music so loud?... I was in the healing line and one of the ushers moved me and I got put in the end." I'm sorry. *Stuff happens.*

Just go kill the giant. Go and get the land that God has promised you.

Let me tell you about Katherine. Katherine drove up from Miami in so much pain she could hardly see. She couldn't take her pain medicine because she wouldn't have been able to drive. She came to one of the morning meetings, and sat in the fifth row. I said, "Everyone who is pain right now, please just stand." About thirty people stood, including Katherine, and I said, "Jesus, touch them all."

About that time, Katherine folded all the way over. Her head went clear down into the chair in front of her. It wasn't a very ladylike position. So I called for the "cover girls" to come and bring the modesty cloths. (We used to call them rag ladies, but they rebelled. So now we call them the Cover Girls of Ignited Church.)

Anyway, back to Katherine. She was left folded over this chair with her derriere in the air for twenty minutes. And I finally thought, "That's enough. She can sit down." I glanced over and she was just easing back into her chair.

Then we learned the rest of her story.

Ten years ago, Katherine was an administrator, managing a huge marketing management firm for Sears, with a number of stores under her command. She was diagnosed with fibromyalgia. In excruciating pain, she had to go on total disability. She was on four major medications that literally eat your body alive, but it was the only way she could function. About six years ago, the fibromyalgia went into a degenerative disease that destroyed her spinal column. Doctors put two six-inch rods in her back, with four bolts holding them, *making it impossible for her to bend.* Ten months before the Outpouring, the degenerative disease went into her hip and doctors gave her a total hip replacement, making it *doubly* impossible for her to bend. She came here for a miracle. And Jesus healed that lady. Nobody ever touched her. She was just healed.

Later X-rays of Katherine's back showed those rods and bolts still in place. But healed, Katherine could bend over normally. Impossible? Not with Jesus.

Do you understand that I don't have the answers? All I know is that *by His stripes we were healed.* It is not right for you to be bound. It is not right for you to have the infirmity. And God wants you to do *anything* you can, *everything* you can to get rid of it.

It was a holy place. It was a holy day. But the woman, bound for eighteen years, didn't even ask Jesus for help. Matter of fact, all we know is that she probably came that day just to worship in the temple. Just to worship

God. Perhaps she had even asked the priests to pray for her many times before, and they had given up.

Perhaps you have had everyone pray for you. And you have almost given up.

I remember one morning at a church in Vancouver, Washington. I'll never forget Teresa, hobbling down the aisle on her crutches, struggling with every step. I just happened to catch her out of the corner of my eye. A friend went to her and said, "Teresa, you need to let the man of God pray for you."

And she said, "No. I don't want to be disappointed again."

Finally, after much urging, Teresa finally came up. She couldn't even stand in the healing line. I came over and prayed for her. She had already had twenty-two surgeries on her legs for cerebral palsy. I didn't know all this. Thank God I didn't know. It would have sucked all the faith right out of me.

Because of the surgeries one of Teresa's legs was physically 2 ¼ inches shorter than the other. And it *grew* in my hand! It was an incredible creative miracle. A couple of days later, she realized she was walking up the stairs without holding on to the railing. A few months after that, Teresa became a bank teller, standing six or eight hours a day.

Now, I don't have the whole story, so shortly I'll have Teresa tell her story—her own powerful, inspiring, humbling, healing story.

But here is the bottom line. If you are bound, get free. If you are sick, get healed. Don't try to figure it out theologically. What if you get disappointed again? Maybe next year is your time. I don't know. Assume that today is your day. *Assume that today is your day.*

Back to Katherine. Do you know what Katherine will tell you? She didn't even come to the morning service to get healed. She came for a little sermon to build her faith so she could get healed at night when Todd prayed for her!

Per capita, there have actually been more healings in the morning service than at night. It is because the night service was just so much **glory** that the speaker sometimes didn't get to pray for all the sick. And we've had just as many people healed in the internet chat room and watching television as we've had in the services.

I don't know *when* God is going to set you free. But you need to plan on it right now. This moment. This instant. *Just receive.*

Eighteen years is too long to be in bondage. So Jesus prayed, "Father, if it be your will, come down and heal this woman, she's an intercessor in the church, and God have mercy on her, and please if it be Your will, oh, God, take away this pain from her life, we beseech You now, O Father." Is that what Jesus said?

He did not! He didn't even pray for the lady. He simply loosed her! "Be *LOOSED* from your infirmity!"

And, by the same token: I command you in the name of the Lord, Jesus Christ, be *loosed* from your infirmity! Be *loosed* from your lack and poverty! Be *loosed* from your improper relationships. Be *loosed* from your ungodly soul ties. Be *loosed* from the demonic powers that have held you captive. Be *loosed*! Be *loosed* in Jesus Name. By His stripes, we were healed. We were made whole.

Building Your Own Faith to Maintain Your Healing

Teresa will tell you that the symptoms didn't go away immediately. As a matter of fact, it was months. She would come into agreement, and then the enemy would try to steal her healing. She'd call and we'd pray again.

Often times when you get healed through a gift of healing, the enemy will try to come back. It is very easy, once some symptoms return, to think, "Oh, I guess I didn't get healed after all," and just give up. And you *will* lose your healing, right then and there. You have to keep your mind stayed on God, stayed on your healing. You have to have your vessel full of God.

If you got your miracle because of somebody else's faith, you now must build your own faith to keep *the miracle that you got from somebody else's faith!* Build your own faith. That is what Teresa had to do. For months, she focused on building her own faith to maintain her healing. She kept her mind stayed on God.

No one knows why everyone isn't healed every time. There are some answers, but there is so much more we do not have an answer for.

But I *do* know this: By His stripes we were healed. I know that the Holy Spirit is here. I know that people were—and are still being—healed. And I know that as you place your petitions before the King of Glory, He says, "Ask and you shall receive, that your joy may be full." Be thankful, however your healing manifests.

God wants to touch you right now. Just receive. And the miracles will start. The moment you feel God touch you, just respond in some way. Don't try to figure it out. *Just receive it.*

Is it a cold wind, is it a hot wind? *Just receive it!*

Do you not feel anything? *Just receive it!*

Maybe you don't feel it because God is taking out something bad and putting in something good. *Just receive it!*

Let your spirit man tune in to the Voice of the Spirit. *Just receive it!*

Bondage of every form, go! It is not *right* that you have been bound with this infirmity. Let it go. Be loosed right now. *Just receive it!*

The breath of God is blowing through you now. Let it wash over you. *Just receive it!*

Be loosed from bondage! Replace it with joy. Replace it with victory. *Just receive it!*

Receive. Receive. Receive. *In Jesus name, receive it now!* Amen.

**"Lakeland Arena - Eduardo Juarez asks
Todd to pray for his daughters"**
Photo by Wes Roderick

"Lakeland Arena - Crowd"
Photo by Wes Roderick

"Lakeland Arena - Roy Fields leading worship"
Photo by Wes Roderick

"Lakeland Arena - Crowd worshipping"
Photo by Stephen R. Strader

"Open Field - Todd Bentley exhorting the crowd"
Photo by Wes Roderick

"Open Field - Crowd worshipping"
Photo by Stephen R. Strader

"Ignited Church - Crowds line up for hours to get inside"
Photo by Wes Roderick

"Ignited Church - Roy Fields leading worship"
Photo by Wes Roderick

"Ignited Church - Todd Bentley and Stephen R. Strader reading praise reports" *Photo by Wes Roderick*

**"Ignited Church -
Stephen Strader
interview testimonies"**
Photo by Wes Roderick

**"Ignited Church -
Todd Bentley and Stephen
Strader interview testimonies"**
Photo by Wes Roderick

**"Ignited Church - Todd Bentley
interviewing a testimony"**
Photo by Wes Roderick

**"Ready for Prayer -
Stephen Strader, his wife Janice, sons Jordan and Austin"**
Photo by David Vespa

**"Ignited Church - Todd Bentley and Stephen Strader pray
over the email prayer requests"** *Photo by Wes Roderick*

"Ignited Church - Todd Bentley preaching"
Photo by Wes Roderick

"Ignited Church - Pastor Stephen Strader preaching Sunday AM"
Photo by David Vespa

"Ignited Church - Prayer Line"
Photo by Wes Roderick

"Ignited Church - Morning Service"
Photo by Stephen R. Strader

"Ignited Church - Crowd during worship"
Photo by Stephen R. Strader

**"Auburndale Life Church -
Todd exhorting the crowd"**
Photo by Stephen R. Strader

**"Auburndale Life Church -
Todd exhorting the crowd"**
Photo by Wes Roderick

**"Auburndale Life Church -
Crowd during worship"**
Photo by Wes Roderick

**"Ignited Church - Stephen Strader
exhorting the crowd"**
Photo by Ryan C. Harmening

**"Apostolic Alignment -
Dr. Clarice Fluitt prophesying over Todd"**
Photo by Ryan C. Harmening

**"Lakeland Baseball Stadium -
Crowd fills the stadium"**
Photo by Wes Roderick

**"Lakeland Baseball Stadium -
Crowd fills the stadium"**
Photo by Wes Roderick

**"Lakeland Airport Tent -
Crowd worshipping"**
Photo by Ryan C. Harmening

**"Lakeland Airport Tent -
Prayer for the nations"**
Photo by Ryan C. Harmening

**"Lakeland Airport Tent -
Todd exhorting the crowd"**
Photo by Ryan C. Harmening

**"Lakeland Airport Tent -
Dave Fitzgerald leading worship"**
Photo by Ryan C. Harmening

"Lakeland Airport Tent - Crowd lining up to get into the tent"
Photo by Ryan C. Harmening

"Lakeland Airport Tent - Crowd lining up to get into the tent"
Photo by Ryan C. Harmening

**"Lakeland Airport Tent -
Apostolic Alignment Ceremony"**
Photo by Ryan C. Harmening

**"Lakeland Airport Tent -
Crowd during worship"**
Photo by Ryan C. Harmening

**"Lakeland Airport Tent -
Pastor Stephen and his wife
Janice during worship"**
Photo by Ryan C. Harmening

**"Lakeland Airport Tent -
Todd reading praise reports"**
Photo by Ryan C. Harmening

**"Lakeland Airport Tent -
Crowd during worship"**
Photo by Ryan C. Harmening

Chapter Ten
Healed in the Ladies' Restroom
--Teresa Pemberton

Born six weeks premature, I weighed a mere 4 lbs 10 oz. Within 24 hours I had gone down to three pounds. When I was a couple of days old, I contracted pneumonia and could not breathe. If they took me out of the incubator for only a few seconds I would turn blue. At some point, I went without oxygen long enough that it caused brain damage. The doctors told my parents that I would never walk, never talk, and that I would be mentally retarded. (They later said I'd never ride a bike, never swim, never drive a stick shift, and never carry a baby full term. They were wrong about those things, too.)

At a year, I still could not sit up on my own, and didn't learn to walk until I was two. At three, I was diagnosed with cerebral palsy, caused by damage to the motor area of the brain. I had severe spasticity in my arms and legs, and had to wear braces on both legs. I also began to have seizures from the brain damage. I had to take Phenobarbital three times a day. If I missed one dose, I'd have a seizure.

At five years old, I had my first surgery. Every time I grew a couple of inches, I had to have another surgery because my tendons wouldn't stretch as my legs grew. To date, I have had twenty-two leg surgeries!

God healed my legs at five years old from having to wear braces. Then, at nine years old, I was prayed for to receive healing from the seizures. I went home from the meeting, threw the Phenobarbital in the trash, and never took another one. I never had any withdrawal, and I never had another seizure. (At age twenty, I carried my son a month overdue. By the time he was born, my blood pressure had skyrocketed to 186/124—even then I didn't have a seizure.)

Later, God slowly healed my hands. I now have played the flute for 31 years. I type on the computer. I do ten-key by touch. I am learning the keyboard. In 1993, the orthopedist noted in my medical file, "No cerebral palsy in upper extremities." He is a concert flautist and knew there was no way I could play those instruments with cerebral palsy in my hands! (All this is documented at the medical center in Portland. My files there are over a thousand pages long!)

Still, my legs were a mess. At one point, I went years without any notable miracles in my body. I was prayed for many times with no change. I began to be discouraged and developed a fear of disappointment.

In 1994, I had my last leg surgery. When I came out of the cast, it was worse than when I went in. My left leg was 2¼ inches shorter than my right. My Achilles tendons were so tight that I could not straighten my legs out, and my feet were so painful that I could not sit in a recliner without a pillow under my ankles so that my feet wouldn't touch the footrest.

I went back to the doctor. His report? There's nothing more we can do for you. You have no tendon left to stretch. It's all scar tissue. You're going to be in a wheelchair. Go home and get ready. Get into a house that will accommodate a chair, and I will order it for you. I burst into tears and argued with him. He agreed to try physical therapy one more time.

It didn't work. On a devastating day in January, 1995, the doctor told me I was going to be in a wheelchair for the rest of my life. I sat in my car and sobbed to the Lord, "You've healed me so many times before. Why? How do you get glory from this?"

The Lord answered to me so loudly that I turned to see if He was sitting in the passenger seat. "WHAT MAN CONSIDERS IMPOSSIBLE IS WHERE I EXCEL!"

I began seeking the Lord for healing. A few weeks later, I overheard a phone conversation between our children's pastor, Mila, and her daughter. The daughter was talking about a meeting she'd been in the night before where even the teenagers and children where touched by God. Several had been on the floor for hours just laughing in the presence of the Lord.

I became very excited! I grabbed her arm. "Is it Rodney Howard-Browne?" I asked. Years before, I had been in a Rodney Howard-Browne meeting in Salem, Oregon, and lay on the floor for over two hours, laughing. I had gone on to laugh throughout the night in my sleep. The Lord told me I was going to laugh till every bone in my body was healed.

She couldn't remember the name of the evangelist, but that he traveled with Rodney Howard-Browne.

That's when I first met Pastor Stephen Strader!

I raced home from the church and hurried to the meeting. The first night, nothing significant happened. I bought a little book on the anointing and took it home to my husband, Aaron. He had been in ministry, but had become so discouraged and disillusioned that he'd quit. He was full of bitterness and almost never went to church.

However, just a few weeks before the meeting with Pastor Stephen, Aaron had actually attended church with me. That day, it was spoken over him that God was preparing him to work a miracle in me.

So, Aaron read the book. And I went off to the meetings again.

Freedom from Fear of Disappointment

Tuesday morning, they had an altar call for freedom from fear. I had developed such a fear of disappointment regarding healing after being prayed for so many years and nothing happening. So intense was the fear that I was afraid to ask for healing. I was in such bondage to this fear that I *could not* release my grip on the pew to go to the altar. But later that night, the pastor's wife prayed and broke that fear off me.

After the meeting I bought Pastor Stephen's tapes on the anointing and took them home. Next morning, Aaron took the tapes to work.

In his small security guard shack, he closed the door and window and began listening to the tapes. The anointing filled the guard shack. A trucker came to go through his gate, and Aaron opened the window to talk to him—and nothing but tongues came out! The trucker says, "I'll have what you're drinking!"

That afternoon, Aaron came home. "Get ready!" he said. "We're going to church!" That night as he set one foot in the door of the church, his entire body started shaking. All through the worship service, he closed his eyes and raised his hands, lost in the presence of the Lord. He was shaking and vibrating so much that he shook the entire pew! He looked at me and said, "I think we're having an earthquake." Everyone around us started laughing because he didn't even know it was him.

Breaking the bondage of bitterness and fear

Pastor Stephen made a beeline for Aaron that night. He pulled him out in the aisle and began to pray over him, speaking into him and breaking off all those years of bondage, bitterness, and unforgiveness. My husband hit the floor, totally free! Pastor Stephen then prayed over me, and I landed right beside my husband.

The next morning Aaron awoke with such joy and freedom—his eyes shining as he went off to work.

I returned to the meeting, excited over what God had done. I knew there was more. At the end of the service, the pastor's wife asked for prayer. After Pastor Stephen prayed over her, and was picking up his Bible to leave, my hand shot up in the air. "Please pray for my legs." My fear of disappointment had truly been broken! I finally had courage enough to ask for my healing.

He asked, "What do the doctors say is wrong with you?" Then he sat me on the front pew, had people come and stand behind him, and watch over his shoulder. As He prayed, the power of God began to vibrate from the top of my head down my body. That night, my leg grew out two whole inches, to within a 1/4 of an inch of normal! It was a creative miracle!

The pain was instantly gone. Instantly!

Before Stephen prayed, I had been on prescription medication every day of my life. I could not walk up and down stairs, except to put one foot up and then drag the next foot up to it, and then do it again. If I was going down the stairs, I had to sit down and scoot. I couldn't balance; the pain in my heels was intense. I'd stand and fall backwards.

Over the next couple of weeks, God slowly adjusted my body. I went off all pain medicine and began being able to stand and walk without help. I could go up and down stairs normally. In May, 1998, I went back to work. In September of 1998 I took a job as a bank teller, standing on my feet as much as eight hours a day. I considered it lack of faith in my healing if I sat down to work. (Now I'm a little smarter!)

Satan never leaves you alone, though. A few years later, in 2004, I blew a disc in my neck and had to have a cervical fusion in C6-C7. Then, in October of 2007, I was in a car accident. I didn't think I was injured. But nine days later, I woke up with a stiff neck that lasted for two months. By the first part of January, I was in so much pain that I couldn't put my head on a pillow.

On March 6, 2008, after an MRI, the doctors informed me that I had spinal stenosis. As they described it, it is where the spinal column collapses onto the spinal cord. Instead of being round, the spinal canal was almost flat. I had almost no spinal fluid in the top part of my spine, hence the spinal headaches. The doctors also informed me that it appeared that the fusion done in 2004 was no longer solid. The disc above it had a huge bone spur on it, and the disc above that one had completely blown out the side, leaving bone and tissue up against my spinal cord. I was looking at surgery, possible triple fusion with two steel plates in my neck.

By this time I was in so much pain, I could hardly function. The doctors took me off work to await surgery. My body began to shut down. My hands and arms felt like they were on fire. I lost almost all use of my hands. I lost thirty percent of the use of my legs, already weak from cerebral palsy and those twenty-two surgeries. I was in serious trouble. *Surgery to remove and reconstruct my backbone was scheduled for May 13, 2008.* I was sent home to wait.

God had other plans.

In early April, a healing outpouring started at Pastor Stephen's church in Lakeland. Pastor Stephen emailed us reports of miracles, then let us know that the services were going live on the internet. We wanted to fly down there, but didn't have the $1,500 we needed to go. So we told the Lord about it and asked Him to provide.

One day, I got a call from Heidi Morter, a lady I'd just met in our new church. "Teresa," she said, "God told me that if I would take you to Lakeland, you'd get healed."

After several days of talking and praying while her husband flew to Lakeland to check it out, this wonderful woman booked tickets to Lakeland. She and I, together with our Pastors Ron and Heidi Thomason, (and, later in the week, Aaron) flew to Lakeland. What these wonderful friends did for me reminds me of the man whose family let him down through the roof to Jesus!

Heidi kept saying, "Teresa, you're going to come home and cancel the surgery." I kept thinking, "I can't, I have to do everything the doctor says, or I won't have a job." I was back, struggling with the fear: what if nothing happens? My friends, who spent all this time and money to take me to Lakeland, will be so disappointed.

I had more fear than faith at that point, but as we set foot on the plane on April 27, I heard the Lord say, "So it begins!"

The plane ride for me was miserable. My pain medicine was in the overhead compartment and everyone around me was asleep. I was in so much pain. An hour and a half out of Atlanta, I was draped over the tray table, sobbing because of the pain.

Waiting in line for 45 minutes that evening, I was in intense pain and began to cry again. My pastors and friend prayed. After we found seats, they went down to worship at the front, and I just sat in my seat. The pain continued throughout the service and I cried several times. Some of it in self pity.

Tuesday morning, we got to be in a service at Ignited Church—our first time in Pastor's Stephen's church. We had not been able to sit under his ministry since 1999, and had only talked on the phone. Then the best news: Pastor Stephen was preaching that morning!

He talked about healing. I became excited as I heard him begin to share testimonies and knew he was going to share mine from 1995. Then he revealed something I'd never heard him tell before—the part about having a fear of disappointment caused by receiving prayer so many times and having nothing happen.

As he shared it, God spoke to me. "You're doing it again," He said. "I didn't disappoint you then, and I won't disappoint you now."

The instant I heard that I knew I was going home healed! I was fearful of going up for prayer, because I thought that if others saw me in the healing line, right after he'd shared about my healing, it would kill their faith. But, later, the Lord told me to take a step and just get down there where the anointing was and soak in it. As I stood down there watching Pastor Stephen pray for people, he saw me and called me to the front. He prayed over me again. "God, just remove every trace of cerebral palsy. Complete the work you already started and launch her into the destiny you've called her to. Complete it, and let it be today, Lord." And I knew that I would be healed that day.

That evening, we went to the Lakeland Center Arena again for service. I was *not* going to have a pity party that night. I decided to just plug in to worship and just love the Lord. As we were singing, "GLORY! GLORY! GLORY!" the atmosphere was charged with the Holy Spirit. It felt like you could reach out and take handfuls of it.

Suddenly, my entire body began to shake in the presence of the Lord. I knew something was about to happen. The Lord said, "Take a step. Get down on the floor and get in it, like you did this morning."

It was a frustrating dilemma. I was sitting in the second section of the balcony. My friends were all down in front worshiping. There were no handrails. I couldn't get down to the floor. I was like the man at the pool of Bethesda. As I was praying, the Lord told me to kill my pride and ask one of the thousand people sitting around me to help me down.

As I looked up, both my Heidi's were charging up the balcony stairs. "Teresa!" they yelled.

"I know!" I said. "It's time. I have to get down there." I was shaking so powerfully under the power of the Holy Spirit that they had to hold me up. As we started down to the floor, I unbelievably had to ask them to stop first at the restroom! I'd been sitting up there for 2 ½ hours, unable to leave the arena. As I stood by the exit door of the restroom (all the while shaking under the power of God), I heard the Lord say "Jump!"

I hadn't been able to jump before, because my left knee was bone on bone. The doctors had told me I needed a knee replacement but I wasn't old enough to receive one. Knee replacements last only a limited number of years, they said, so I needed to wait ten more years for one.

But I heard the Lord say, "Jump!" And, without giving it a thought, I jumped. When my feet hit the floor, I was healed. All the pain left my body and I could move my head, up down and all around. I could even touch my chin to my chest, something that was medically impossible with the bones fused in my neck.

God healed me in the Ladies Restroom, without anyone laying hands on me!

As we went out in the hall, I ran up and down the hall, and jumped around. I even got yelled at by the security guard for running in the halls. When we got to the stage, we found out that even the bathroom delay was in God's timing.

As we got to the stage, Todd Bentley was talking to a guy and his mom on the other side. He turned and asked me what I was healed of. I said "Spinal stenosis and cerebral palsy."

"Spinal stenosis?" He whirled around to the guy on the other side of the stage, "Didn't you just say your mom needed healing from spinal stenosis?" He said yes. "Bring her up here!" Todd stood her in front of me and commanded, "*You* pray for her!" As I prayed, I felt a column of fire come down over both of us. The lady was completely healed!

On the night I was healed, I literally went walking, leaping and praising God. I ran up and down stairs, walked up without handrails, and jumped over and over again. NO PAIN! I went back to the hotel and dumped my pain medication down the toilet. I haven't needed anything more than ibuprofen since then.

The Big Test

The day after we got back from Lakeland, May 6, I had a pre-op appointment. I was extremely nervous about telling my doctor that I had been to a revival and gotten healed. As I stepped out of the car, the Lord spoke, "It's time for the doctors to stop being law. For your entire life, their word has been law. Their word is not law. I AM LAW."

Immediately, I answered, "Yes, Lord!"

As the doctor came into the exam room, I discovered that it was not my surgeon but another doctor, someone I'd not met before. He said, "I'm here to tell you about your surgery, check your health, and answer any questions you might have."

"And I'm here to tell you that you're going to get a surprise when you get in there!"

He gave me a strange look, and began addressing the fact that my blood pressure was high, at 164/121. I told him, "That's just because I'm excited!"

He asked what I was excited about. So I said, "Have you heard what's happening in Lakeland?" (My favorite question right now.) He said no. "There is a great healing revival going on there and God told my friends if they took me, I'd get healed, so we went and I got healed."

A blank mask dropped over his face. I could hear the thought,

"This lady's wacko!" I told him that I was not the only one who got healed—that one lady had steel rods dissolve in her back, another one still has the rods, but could bend any way she wanted, and that another lady got healed of spinal stenosis at the same time I was. He wanted to see the x-rays!

He started discussing Lakeland. "How do I get there?" he asked. "Which airport do I fly into? I want to see this for myself." He was astonished that I'd thrown my medication away and didn't need it.

I told him, "God said for us to do whatever the doctor advises." He began running his tests. I passed the first three, but he said, "Not definitive."

Then he gave me the hand grip test. When I had left for Lakeland, the grip in my left hand was less than 7 pounds. The day after I got back, it was 75 pounds. The grip in my right hand had been less than 24. Now it was 90!

The doctor got a funny look on his face. He took the gripping instrument out of my hand and, after clenching it as hard as he could, he turned it around so I could read his results. His grip was only 82!

He said, "I don't have the authority to cancel the surgery, but I know I wouldn't want my mom or my sister to have their backbone removed if they didn't have to! So I'm going to recommend that they cancel the surgery."

We talked some more about healing. "If you could bottle this, you'd be rich!" he said.

I replied, "I can't sell it, but I'll give it away."

On my birthday, Friday, May 9, he called me at home, and asked how I was doing. Pain free, I told him. They were going to cancel the surgery, but the doctor, being concerned that the healing might go away, was going to keep me on the books for eight weeks, in case.

Eight weeks came and went. I am totally healed and am having a blast sharing with people about healing. The anointing *is* transferable. We are seeing miracles each time I share and each time my husband preaches. On Father's Day, there were seven miracles in the small church we were in. God gets all the Glory!

Teresa and Aaron Pemberton are even now healing others, as they have been healed.

Both of Teresa's doctors have been convinced. With Teresa's permission, they are giving out her name and story to other physicians. God be praised!

And your Olympics coach asks, "Has your faith been built up?"

Chapter Eleven
Setting the Record Straight

In case you have not read the comments on the internet you may not know the incredible amount of hatred and accusations against the Outpouring, Todd Bentley, Fresh Fire Ministries, Ignited Church, and me. That is one of the reasons we felt an imperative to stand with the apostles, and have the Apostolic Alignment. So we could be certain our Biblical backbone was straight.

And now that it has been broadcast that Todd has fallen morally, the critics want to say, "I told you so!" We don't discount that many gave "warnings," but they focused only on the manifestations or doctrines. Not one gave warnings regarding "character."

Remember this. Just because King David fell morally, we did not cut the Book of Psalms out of the Bible. We do not read Psalms with the thought, "A murderer and adulterer wrote these songs." No. We allow David's words to stand in all their purity and longing for God. And they have comforted our hearts for centuries. The man was not pure, but his words were.

Right Judgment

When we are concerned about something, it is foolish for us to ignore red lights, or even caution flags. When we see or receive a "caution," we need to evaluate it, not ignore it. But I feel there is a significant error that people make when they "judge" something based on personal preferences and/or partial or flawed information.

I have to make judgments every day. Is this salesman telling me the truth? Can I trust this repairman? I must judge my children—to correct them and bring them into integrity. I have to judge.

Many people say that the Bible says, "Judge not." Let me correct that.

The Bible doesn't say that; in fact, the Bible tells us to judge. We are to be a "fruit inspector." But we must judge in a proper way.

The Bible says, "Judge not, lest you be judged. *With the same measure of judgment*, you will be judged." So, if I judge you with one standard, but do not judge myself with the same standard, then I become like the Pharisees who put a burden on the people that they themselves could not even carry.

So, when the Bible says, "Judge not," it is not telling us *not* to judge. It is warning us to be careful when we judge other people, that we hold ourselves to a much higher standard. Always judging with a spirit of humility. How do I know if this person is a man or woman of God? I have to take what they say, search the Scriptures, search my heart, and find out if they are living right. I have to judge. I can't just take anybody hook, line and sinker. If I did, I would be naïve.

But to judge something as being not of God, or to judge it as being a sin, or to judge it as being of the devil—if we make that judgment, we have to go to the greatest lengths to follow Biblical patterns. One of those Biblical patterns is that I go to my brother, considering myself lest I also be tempted, and I take a witness with me. If the person still ignores me, *then* I take it to the church. (Check out Galatians 6:1-2, and Matthew 18:15-17. In fact, check out those Scriptures in *The Message Bible* for real "today" wisdom.)

Wrong Judgment

What happens when we make a wrong judgment? (Notice I didn't say "if," but "when.") The principle in Matthew is that you go in a spirit of meekness. The Bible says you always give somebody the benefit of the doubt. And, so, unless you are in a position of authority where you have to make a final ruling, our judgment should always be, "Lord, I give them the benefit of the doubt. I choose not to believe, or I choose to be uncomfortable with what they are doing. So I'm just going to leave them in your hands."

For example, if I'm watching a television preacher and I am uncomfortable with his method or his style, I don't say that he is of the devil or that he is wrong. I just say, "This is not for me," and I leave it alone. I don't get up in my pulpit and say, "So-and-so is of the devil." I might say, "I'm uncomfortable with the choices they have made. I prefer to make these other choices, and here is why." Or, "I am uncomfortable, and here is why." But I would avoid publicly saying anything until I had contacted the person and dialogued with them.

Obviously, if I am a sitting judge, or if I have been asked to make a final decision—say, if two church members come in and I am asked, as pastor, to make a judgment decision, I have to make it. Right or wrong, I must do it.

What is God's reaction if I'm wrong? If your heart is pure to the best of your ability and you made a decision, God knows the position of your heart. God withholds judgment against you because you made a decision based on the information you were given.

How many times have you misjudged somebody, just based on their appearance, or maybe one little thing they said? Or you did not have all the information or background. Let me tell you this: we never have all the information. Only God has all the information. That is why we must be so very, very careful in our judgments.

If you discover you've made a wrong judgment, you must ask the person to forgive you for wronging them, same as in any other instance. You must go through the process.

Prophet Doodad

Let me play the critics' advocate for a moment. Let's say "Prophet Doodad" is going to come speak. If someone were to tell me beforehand, "Hey, I understand that Prophet Doodad is struggling with alcoholism, and I heard that twenty years ago he was actually caught in adultery as a homosexual." From that bit of gossip I'll be predisposed to think that this prophet has the possibility of controversy in his life. When he steps into the pulpit, I'm going to be watching for any little sign of a flaw.

That is exactly, in my opinion, the problem with most critics and "heresy hunters." They have a predisposition of, "I've got to watch every evangelist for something wrong." Let's lay the cards on the table. Do you know of any great revivalists in the past or present who haven't had elements of controversy about something? You can go right down the line with many of the great men or women of God, and many have had some flaws or mistakes, made poor decisions, or had issues of character or personality. They are human. But, if you are already predisposed to think that every great man or woman of God is going to have flaws, and you go into a meeting with that on your mind, you will look up there and find them really quick.

One of the significant problems is with the medium of the internet. What happened is that people simply went ahead and published their opinions on their websites, which is essentially taking it to the world. Some leaders stood up in their pulpits and expressed their "serious concerns" about what was happening here in Florida, and they never even called me. Nor wrote a letter of concern—even though they had access to my contact information. That is wrong, in my opinion, because *they have violated Scripture in criticizing somebody whom they feel is violating Scripture!*

I once responded to a castigating e-mail from a woman asking, "Is there any possibility, based on the fact that *so* many people believe that the Outpouring is real, and that what is happening here in Lakeland is real, do you at least admit there is a possibility that you've misunderstood something or there is something you are not seeing? She said, "Absolutely not. This is wrong. You are the one who has missed it."

At that point, I think she crossed the line, because you don't call unclean what God has declared to be clean. And I think that is what she did. And that is why I labeled her, based on that response, a "heresy hunter." Had she said, "Anything is possible, but I don't think so," that would have been fine. But not admitting the possibility that you could be wrong, or that you may have misunderstood, when you are not in a position of authority to make a final judgment—I think that is a wrong thing.

That is my beef with many of the critics and "heresy hunters." To this day, they have not bothered to ask the questions. Even this lady I was talking about only sent accusations in the form of questions. And she was angry with me because I would not answer accusations. I *will* answer any honest questions that you have, but I refuse to answer accusations. I don't have to defend anybody or anything. I will always be ready to give an answer for the Hope that is within me. But I am not going to answer an accusation. An accusation concealed as a question is still an accusation.

I have found that anyone who came to the meetings with an open heart - and notice I did *not* say *open mind* - discovered what all of us have experienced... THIS IS A WORK OF GOD. Yes, there was a mixture of flesh and Spirit. The Bible says there is a war between the flesh and the Spirit. The truth is: I don't know of a choir in any church in the world that doesn't have flesh and Spirit mixture! But they can still be anointed.

Please know that, in these kinds of meetings, there is a lot of flesh, "muddy water." That is simply the nature of an outpouring. But I want you to know that from Day One, we worked diligently to clean away every semblance of flesh. We wanted the stream of Holy Spirit to flow clear and free. From Day One we declared and decreed:

I declare that this Outpouring will be a pure Gospel.

I declare that it will be a true Light.

I declare that it will not be anything anti-Christ.

I declare that it will be direct from the throne of Heaven.

I declare and decree that the people who are hungry for God and who are asking God for something to eat from Heaven's table will receive the bread of life, not a stone, not a serpent, but healthy food, true food from the very kitchen of Heaven.

I declare and decree that everybody will be healed. Everybody will be saved. Everybody will be delivered.

We bind any power of the enemy that would try to distract and confuse.

I declare and decree that the Kingdom of God is being established in the hearts of the men and the women that receive this Outpouring into their life.

That they have eyes to see, ears to hear, and God give us all discernment.

Protect us from the evil one.

In the name of the Lord Jesus Christ, I establish it now, in the Name of Jesus.

And, once the Apostolic Alignment of June 23 took place, God was able to reveal some of the carnal activities that were going on behind the scenes, cleansing the Outpouring, just as we have continuously and constantly decreed.

Chapter Twelve
The Rock of Offense

Each one of the different outpourings has had what I call the "rock of offense." In the charismatic movement, they called it the "red door." There was something that you had to look past, something you had to get around, in order to get what you wanted.

For the Charismatics, if you wanted the Gifts of the spirit you had to deal with speaking in tongues—which was the rock of offense, the red door. Unfortunately, in the early days of Pentecost, tongues became the goal. So, if a Catholic or Methodist or Baptist wanted the spirit of God, they had to get past the tongue issue. Once you got on the other side of the red door, you realized how many wonderful "gifts" were inside. It was the Charismatics who taught us that speaking in tongues was the *door*, not the *goal*.

God is the goal. Relationship is the goal. Intimacy is the goal. Sensitivity to the Holy Spirit is the goal. It's all these other issues—these rocks of offense or red doors—that stand in the way.

While it sounds holy to say that God is the goal, the more accurate thing to say is that the goal is what God is putting on the table. For example, when God put Pentecost back on the table in the early 1900's, the Pentecost *experience* was the goal.

And here is the "rock of offense" that we have to get around today: The passion of this Outpouring is to experience God in every way that God has ever expressed Himself. The Gift of the Spirit have not yet been fully experienced! Certainly we can say that THIS generation hasn't seen what happened in some of the great awakenings or revivals of the past.

When you hear someone from the Outpouring recounting the ministries of A.A. Allen and William Branham, we are saying, "I want those gifts."

We're not talking about their personalities, or their weaknesses, or their character issues. We're talking about "whatever God did for William Branham and A.A. Allen, God can do for me." This Outpouring has put a passion in our lives for whatever anybody has *ever* experienced from God—whether in the Bible or in history—and we want to experience it, as well.

God has *MORE* for us than we've ever experienced. Are we going to limit God? I don't think so.

Think about this: how many people with a fundamentalist background do not believe that miracles are for today? Oh, they say, "If it's in the Word, we believe it." Yet you can show them Scripture until you are breathless— the tongues, the gifts, the healings in the Bible—and they absolutely have chosen not to believe. It is precisely like the old adage, "A man convinced against his will is of the same opinion still." Rarely will you ever convince anyone just by showing them the Word.

It appears that one of the best ways to convince someone is through an experience. Once they have an *experience*, then they'll be open to receiving the *doctrine*. Bishop Clarice Fluitt taught me, "God gives you an experience; then God gives you doctrine."

The first time she said it, I didn't like it. I am a Word man; my Dad is a Word man. She took me aback. So when Bishop Clarice said, "God gives you an experience, then God gives you doctrine," I thought, "Why can't we find it in the Word, and then experience it?" But it now appears to me that it is just the opposite most of the time. You have the experience, then you find it in the Word, *then* you believe it, utterly.

Here is a case in point: Peter. It was all through the Word of God that the Gospel would be to the Jews *and* the Gentiles. Look at how many prophetic words there are throughout the whole old covenant that the Gospel was going to be preached to the heathens. Jesus Himself preached to the Jew first, then to the Greek, and so on.

Yet Peter and the other disciples were totally focused on the Jews. Even though it was *in* the Word, it took an *experience,* a vision of a sheet coming down out of Heaven with the unclean animals, to break it. — *"Do not call unclean what I have declared to be clean. Arise, kill and eat."*

116

Bishop Clarice shared some amazing personal experiences that served to strengthen her faith in God's Word. The *experience* made all the difference.

When her daughter Cathy was only four years old, the little finger on her right hand was accidentally cut off at the first joint. After much intense prayer, the Lord performed a creative miracle, restoring bone, fingertip and fingernail. Now, for me, that would certainly have been enough experience to believe from the depths of my being.

But the Lord was not done yet. At another time, Bishop Clarice's 12-year-old son, Trey, was critically burned when battery acid exploded on his face and body as he was playing outside their home. Within eight hours after prayer and listening to a testimony of the miraculous healing experienced by a woman named Betty Baxter, Trey's faith was accelerated to believe God for total healing. There was not a scar or burn left anywhere—even though the doctors had diagnosed him with second and third degree burns. Much later still, her 18-year-old daughter Rebecca was thrown from a horse and repeatedly stomped. Again, after much prayer, Rebecca was totally restored—without scars—*within eighteen hours*.

Now, of course, when Bishop Clarice reads the Word, there is absolutely no question about her believing utterly and receiving the doctrine of miracles and healings. It is richly reflected in her life and ministry— and in the myriads of people who have been healed through her. The information became revelation and produced transformation. Thank God for an "experience."

It is *ALL* about the Presence of God

Your spirit man has senses, just as your physical body has senses— hearing, seeing, touch, smelling, taste.

Your spirit man can taste: "Oh, taste and see that the Lord is good."[24]

Your spirit man can hear: "I'll let you in on the sweet old truths, stories we heard from our fathers, counsel we learned at our mother's knee. We're not keeping this to ourselves, we're passing it along to the next generation—

---

24 Psalm 34:8   (KJV)

God's fame and fortune, the marvelous things he has done."[25]

Your spirit man can smell: "...fragrant cedar branches are the beams of our house, and pleasant smelling firs are the rafters."[26]

Your spirit man can touch: "He touched my mouth with the coal and said, 'Look. This coal has touched your lips. Gone your guilt, your sins wiped out.'"[27]

Your spirit man can see: "I will pour out my Spirit on every kind of people: Your sons will prophesy, also your daughters; your young men will see visions, your old men dream dreams. When the time comes, I'll pour out my Spirit..."[28]

And, your spirit man can feel. "Everyone who cares for truth, who has any *feeling* for the truth, recognizes my voice."[29] *What are you feeling?*

What are you feeling?

When Todd Bentley interviewed people, he would say, "Tell me what you *felt* when the healing power touched you!" He loved to hear that, and would ask it over and over. He truly wanted to know *what* you felt in the touch of God. He's been criticized for being so focused on how people felt, but it is his passion.

Every man or woman of God who is worth their salt is passionate about some facet of God. If you are in Rhinehart Bonke's presence for thirty seconds you will hear his passion for Africa. "It must be saved!" Marilyn Hickey's passion is the study of the Word of God. In her presence, you will hear that you need to have the Word of God in your heart, to study it, to memorize it.

The often-repeated message from the platform of this Outpouring has been the Presence of God—and experiencing God in as many different ways as possible. It comes right out of the story of Moses having communication with God: "We appreciate the fact that you are going to give us an angel to lead us, God. But unless YOUR Presence goes with us, we ain't going. We are not moving from this spot."

25 Psalm 78:1	The Message
26 Song of Solomon 1:17	NLT
27 Isaiah 6:7	The Message
28 Acts 2:14	The Message
29 John 18:37	The Message

That is the part that people miss about this Outpouring. It's not about the miracles. It's not about the healings. It's not about the angels. It is all about the Presence of God. To become Presence driven. To be led by the Spirit. To be intimate with the Spirit. To experience God and His Presence and His Glory, in any way, shape or form that anybody ever has. To have the same supernatural experience of the Holy Spirit that other historical figures had, so that we can have the authority and power to win souls and see signs and wonders and miracles, just like they did. The *holy* part, not the bad character parts and not the heretical parts. We want only the *holy* part.

The way I explain it to people is this: If you want the passion for worship that King David had from the time he was a youngster, singing songs to the sheep, writing the book of Psalms, being a man after God's own heart, you say, "I would like to have a heart like David had." You are *NOT* asking for David's adultery, or misjudgments, or the spirit of murder when he sent Uriah out to the battlefront to be killed, or to be a horrible parent. You are asking for the holy part.

From that standpoint, this is exactly what we're doing. We're asking God for the same mantle to come upon us that the Apostle Paul had, so we can get revelation of Scripture. We're asking for the same mantle as Billy Graham, to walk into stadiums and call people to repentance. We want the anointing that William Branham had, to be able to operate in the Words of Knowledge. We want the same mantle as A.A. Allen, to have the boldness of faith. We want the same anointing as John G. Lake, to walk in the Presence of God. Like Kathryn Kuhlman, we want to step into a room and watch the miracles happen.

The Bible says, "Seek ye first the kingdom of God and His righteousness." As long as we walk in humility, as long as we are holding steadfastly to the principles of Jesus Christ, as long as we are exalting Jesus Christ, as long as we are utilizing whatever anointings we are given to further the Kingdom of God and not to bring attention to ourselves, I believe we are in integrity with God.

So, in my opinion, anybody who says this Outpouring was not of God is totally basing it on false information and/or misinformation.

We would worship God for ninety minutes or two hours, literally on our faces, in the most incredible worship one has ever experienced in his life, with the Spirit of God putting goose bumps on your arms, literally feeling the air charged with Holy Spirit. And then some misguided person says, "Did you see that lady over there shaking? I think she has a demon. This whole outpouring is demonic because that lady is over there, shaking."

You see how dumb that is? Every service started off with prayer, dedicating this service to Jesus Christ, putting it all under His Power, teaching out of Scripture, praising God—how can one misjudge something so badly? To me, it did not compute.

The Wheat and the Tares

Remember Jesus' parable about the wheat and tares? The farmer scattered seed on some fertile ground and it started to grow great, big, healthy wheat. Then, somebody who hated the farmer sneaked in one night and tossed around some weed seeds. Suddenly, there are all these nasty weeds in that great, big, lovely field of wheat. And the farmer's workers come running to tell the farmer. Shall we pull it all out?

"No," the wise farmer answered. "You'll uproot the wheat if you do."[30] *Let both grow together until the harvest. Then I will tell the harvesters to sort out the weeds, tie them into bundles, and burn them, and to put the wheat in the barn.*

Brilliant parable, Jesus. Such common sense within the sacred wisdom.

The principle of the wheat and tares—as it correlates to the Outpouring— is like a kindergarten class full of eager children whose teacher gives them an assignment. "Okay, class, let's draw a picture of our family." Each child will draw something different. Some will draw stick figures. Others might have a little more detail, but not much. Some will draw all the people in their families, and even the family dog. Some may even draw the neighbor's dog. If the teacher has an ounce of sensitivity, he will praise whatever the child has done. The teacher will not likely say, "Oh, you got it all wrong. That dog is not a part of your family!" The object is to get everybody drawing, and everyone's drawing gets celebrated!

Later, perhaps when the student gets to the fourth or fifth grade, the teacher will begin to give critiques to help the child become more mature and

30 Matthew 13:29-30

sophisticated in his artwork. "Let's shade in a bit here," or "Take a look at how a nose actually grows." More is required as the child matures. It was the same for the Outpouring. As the meetings matured, more was required.

In the Outpouring, the first objective was to get everyone experiencing God! In whatever way the Holy Spirit wanted them to experience it! Not in some old way that we dredged up as *outward holiness*. This Outpouring's experiences were all so obviously fresh and new. The parable of the wheat and tares is precisely why Todd and I said, "We are not going to control this. We are not going to try to correct everything and make everything *nice, neat, and safe.*"

Number one, we didn't know everything that the Holy Spirit wanted to accomplish. If we tried to make things *nice*, we could be pulling up the wheat instead of the tares. *Nice* can kill the anointing. All you need to do is look at history and you will see it over and over and over again. When we try to control the anointing, it dies.

Sometimes, people get caught up in "yesterday's" anointings. Years ago, there was a revival in India. An unusual thing happened. The Indians began to clap and bounce in their seats and clap faster and faster and faster, and work themselves into a frenzy, and then the Power would fall. And they would get the Holy Spirit. To this day, over fifty years later, many in the classical Pentecostal groups still do it. They beat a little drum, clap really fast, and lather themselves into a frenzy. When the Holy Spirit tries to do something different or new, they are very slow to embrace it. Many of us are just like this.

Go to certain churches here in America and the folks don't feel like they've had church until they have worked themselves up...spinning, jerking, jumping, laughing, crying. Why are they doing this? I believe that many are trying *to recapture* something wonderful that happened years ago.

It is the same as Moses keeping the veil on his face too long. Remember? When Moses came down from the mountain, he had to put a veil on his face because the glory was too bright to behold. But when the glory started to fade, he kept the veil on, because he was embarrassed and didn't want the folks to know.

When the glory lifts, take the veil off! Don't walk around with a veil pretending you still have the glory! Wait for and enjoy whatever the Holy Spirit wants to give you at *this* moment.

We are all challenged at one time or another to try to maintain faded glory. And I understand it, truly I do. We all want that passionate, personal experience of God. Perhaps you don't think the Holy Spirit has touched you until you jerk or move or laugh or cry. The manifestation of the Holy Spirit isn't necessarily in a laugh, or a jerk, or a *boom bang shambah yabba dabba doo*. You don't have to fall down every time. As Bishop Clarice says, "We should learn to contain our vessel. When God overtakes us we will yield; we should not need to give a 'courtesy fall' to appear spiritual. Keep it real."

Many of the services in this Outpouring have been very different. One service, every hair on your body would be standing on end, with your goose bumps moving aside to make room for new goose bumps. The air would be like stepping into a hydroelectric tank. The next service might turn out to be completely different—laughter, perhaps. Another service might find us face down on the floor, worshipping in complete humility. It was whatever the Holy Spirit wanted to give *at that moment*.

Take the veil off. Just worship. And when the Holy Spirit gives you something, accept it fresh. *You* don't have to *make* something happen. Just receive and enjoy what the Holy Spirit is doing.

I have been amazed at how many people find one kind of manifestation of the Spirit very acceptable and others feel it is demonic. Or, at best, they feel it is *not necessary*. "This is not God," they say. "Do it differently, like we used to." The truth is that each generation inevitably becomes legalistic and outwardly holy about its own special outpouring. "This is the best and only way to experience God."

Could you imagine going into the local buffet where they have multiple serving tables filled with a large variety of food, and you see a food you just don't eat. You call for the manager of the restaurant. "Sir, you are serving liver and onions. I don't eat them. Please *remove* them now so I can eat." I can see his face now! He probably will tell you to *just don't eat them. Leave them alone.*

So. When you go to that *spiritual* buffet that God often serves in any given service, leave the liver and onions alone. And whatever you do, do *not* eat the beets. Beets and liver are of the devil!!!! Leave 'em alone. Don't tell the manager about them. He doesn't care. Don't tell me about them. I don't care.

Now, hear my heart. My words are being funny. I do care. Behind the scenes we were continually correcting things, making adjustments, and taking care of things. But normally, we were not going to stop a certain manifestation so you could feel comfortable.

Here is the cardinal point of the wheat and the tares. In the heat of the moment, sometimes words don't come out right. There *are* going to be things said, or points not explained. Even *I* don't agree 100% with everything that I say! I go home after a service and my wife will tell me, "You shouldn't have said that." And I hang my head and grovel. "I'm sorry." Or I may come home and rewind the service and review all the ways I could have done it better.

I'm sure you have experienced something similar in your life. Just leave it. If you can improve or do it better next time, good. Let the wheat and weeds grow together. When the Harvester comes, He'll sort it out. Just let it go. It's going to be okay.

Just know this. We want *YOU* to eat and drink. We have plenty of men and women of God telling us what to do. Take off your badge that says "revival police." Take it off. Just drink. Get healed. Get delivered. Get set free. Then go back to your church, and do it the way God tells you to do it! Fresh!

Seeing Things Differently

There will be people that, no matter what you say, are not going to comprehend what you are talking about. Have you ever watched Fox News? They show you two sides, the right and the left, and the commentators are debating, arguing, yelling—usually over the top of each other. They won't even listen. If you ask James Carvell about President George Bush's administration, you will get one answer.[31] If you ask Sean Hannity, you are going to get a different response.[32] Two intelligent people, with two diverse opinions. How can they see it so differently?

---

31 James Carvell is an American "far left" political consultant and commentator.
32 Sean Hannity is an American conservative political commentator.

Do you understand? That is why we have Baptist and Methodists and Catholics and Pentecostals. It's because two intelligent people see the same thing two different ways. Who knows who is correct? Maybe both are wrong. But our prayer should always be: God, show me. Take it away if it is wrong.

If I were ever to sit on a television set across from Bill O'Reilly[33] or Larry King[34], answering criticisms about the Outpouring, I know exactly what I would say. "If I am a person of integrity, sir, I would be willing to pray this prayer: 'God, if there is anything You want me to have, give it to me. If there is anything You don't want me to have, take it away.'" And that *is* my fervent and constant prayer.

For this Outpouring, as well as for everything else in our lives, that should be our honest prayer. *"God, if there is anything You want me to have, give it to me. If there is anything You don't want me to have, take it away."* With that prayer, we have released trying to figure things out by our human understanding. *"I want Your understanding, Lord. I want what You have to give. And if something is not right or not appropriate, please, just take it away. Release it from my life. I am willing. I am listening to You."*

As humans, especially in the area of our beliefs and religion, we want to feel safe. We want to experience God safely. But you *can't* experience God safely. You have to walk on the water. If you want to experience Christ, you have to walk on the water, knowing that the storm is raging, knowing that your brothers in the boat will think you are a show-off, or think that you are a fool, or think that you've lost your mind, or they'll think that you're a heretic because only Jesus can walk on the water. What makes you think you can do that? But do we forget that Peter actually walked on water? He could do it—so long as he kept his eye on the goal, on Jesus Christ! He sank only *after* he stopped looking at Jesus and started looking at the scary waves.

I want to tell you about a couple that got caught in the cross-hairs of a polite church that was not open to experiencing God in every way that God has ever expressed Himself. Actually meeting them was, in itself, a miracle.

My cohort in this story-telling adventure is Mary Achor. She comes from

33 Bill O'Reilly is an American ultra conservative political commentator.
34 Larry King is an American television/radio personality who hosts a nightly interview program on CNN called Larry King Live.

a different stream of Christianity, but her brother and sister-in-law, Frank and Francee Gordon, have been Pentecostals for about thirty years. Not only that, Frank and Francee had attended one of Todd Bentley's first Open Heaven conferences in Abbottsford in 2003, as well as Todd's first "Healing 101" school in San Jose, California, in 2005.

So, when Mary told them that she was coming to Lakeland for the book, to interview me and to see everything for herself, there was a stunned silence. What would be the odds of that happening? It was obvious that the Holy Spirit had something very important in mind. So Frank and Francee came to Lakeland. I'll let Frank tell their story.

> For some years Francee and I had been traveling to various outpourings around the country, wherever there was a healing ministry. In 2001, a friend asked if we wanted to go to Kansas City to a meeting. Seems there was some guy with a healing ministry coming from Canada. So we drove the two hours to Kansas City, just to check him out. It was, of course, Todd Bentley. The meeting was in a small church. Instead of thousands of people, he was speaking to hundreds.
>
> His heart for God was evident even back then. We decided we wanted more. We would watch Todd's itinerary, and every time he came back to Kansas City, we'd drive up. Then we started going farther afield. We went to a conference in Las Vegas, to Abbottsford once, and then to the healing school in San Jose. These times were very precious to us.
>
> Because of our experiences, we began to accept and believe more and more of God's miracles. And we learned that *healing is transferable.*
>
> One night, we left one of Todd's meetings and drove back to Columbia. We no sooner returned than we heard tragic news. The son-in-law of one of our church pastors had cut his femoral artery playing paintball, as he was kicking in a window in an old abandoned house. Fortunately, one guy on his team was a medic, or he would have died in minutes. Even so, the prognosis was grim. He, a career army paratrooper, was probably going to lose his leg.

Francee and I, and four or five others who regularly went to healing meetings, drove to the hospital to pray for the soldier. We had the faith that he would be totally healed. (Oddly, the pastor and his family did not have that absolute faith. We asked them to step out while the rest of us prayed.)

Francee put oil on his brow, and the soldier told her later, "It was hot, hot, hot." There was a Presence in the room. All the people in that room had the faith to bring the glory down. From the prognosis, that soldier should have died, or lost a leg, or limped the rest of his life. But he had a rapid recovery and restoration of the leg. Nerves were regenerated. Right leg is stronger than the left. He doesn't limp. And he still jumps out of planes. It reminds him every day, he says, of how God rescued him. The doctor says it was a miracle.

God put a vulnerability and hunger in us. It was shared by only a handful of others in our church. It was hard for us to see the other perspective. When you do get that revelation and other people— those whom you respect in your own church—are not on board with you, it's hard to figure out.

Eventually, we had to leave the church we had attended for twenty-five years. They didn't want the Holy Spirit. We no longer belonged there. I prayed and prayed about it, and I'd get a recurring dream, where God would say, "I don't want you there." And I'd pray, "Okay, we're out. Now what? What do you want us to do now?" And the dream would come again, "I don't want you there." It was frustrating.

We finally realized we simply had to wait in the Spirit. We did get into the healing room group and prophetic groups in St. Louis, but even those went away. All of a sudden, we went from being a strong presence in our church, to nothing. Frankly, it has been extremely disheartening.

A friend from St. Louis called about the second week in May and said Todd was on television from the Outpouring. We watched every night. Francee called all our friends, "Want to go to Florida?" Too busy. How could you not go? They didn't even want to turn on the television.

When my sister told us she was going, it seemed like the time to go. We arrived the day after the Apostolic Alignment. Everything was hopping.

In the tent, we felt the Presence of God. If you aren't searching for the Presence of God, you don't go to those kinds of meetings. When that many are there, with that intensity, God is going to pour out his blessing on those who show up. It was a renewal, a refreshing, in Lakeland. The Outpouring was a renewing of our commitment to the things God has in store for us. It was, indeed, a relief.

In the Toronto Blessing, it had been all about refreshing. Enjoying God. Lots of slaying in the spirit. Lots of manifestation of the Holy Spirit. Lakeland was a different kind of anointing, even on the grounds when we arrived.

There was an assurance—instead of being so much under the spirit you can't walk. It seemed deeper, more sacred, more holy. It seemed anointed for a feeling of safety. Camaraderie—the people all around greeted you with such sweet smiles. More of a sovereign power. Heavy. Deep. Holiness. Reverence for God. Quiet unto yourself.

Things are changing. After we returned from Lakeland, we learned that the city and county are not going to renew the contract I'm working under. It gave me a perfect excuse to leave. I'll do something fresh. And, in Lakeland, Francee saw one of the couples from our prophetic group in St. Louis. We'll be going up there in a couple of weeks. We don't know what the next phase is. But we know that in Lakeland God gave us the impetus to move on. We'll find our next step in Spirit with people who want God as much as we do.

One of the reasons why the Outpouring is so powerful: Like Frank and Francee, everybody who is coming *wants* to be here! And has paid a price to be here. And has come as a seeker. Has come with desperation. Has come with the necessity of a miracle. Each has come with the desire to experience God in a fresh, new way.

Chapter Thirteen
Something about Angels

One of the hot topics of the outpouring was about angels. Personally, I've never really thought much about angels. I've never seen an angel or experienced an angel. I have also joked with people, "I don't know about people who see these angels. I think they're a little off, because *I've* never seen an angel, so therefore it can't really be that important!" Joking about it, you know. But I really, kind of, sort of, meant it! Until I had that *experience* of an angel that I told you about earlier. Needless to say, I have been paying a lot more attention to the talk of angels.

There were two basic problems. One problem was the stories of angelic visitations. The second problem was Todd's seeming fascination with William Branham.

William Branham was a great Voice of Healing evangelist who was notable for the fact that wherever he ministered, a healing angel would show up. In his later years of ministry, Branham got off track doctrinally, denying the Trinity and requiring people to be re-baptized in the name of Jesus only. Once, when someone asked where his power to heal came from, Branham replied that it came from his angel. Whenever the angel wasn't present, Branham wouldn't even minister. The critics of William Branham said that he emphasized the angel too much.

Because Todd has mentioned the healing angel as triggering this anointing, and because he has talked about William Branham and A.A. Allen, both of whom arguably ended their ministries in disgrace, critics claim that Todd, too, is now emphasizing angels too much—and that he is claiming to have the same angel that Branham had. So, they say, if Todd has the same angel that Branham had, then he has the same doctrinal problems as well. Let's address that one first. Now that Todd's flaws have been revealed, critics are blaming the character flaws on the angels.

Here is the bottom line. *Our focus is on Jesus Christ.* Not Branham. Not his angel. Nothing else. Jesus Christ, alone.

There is a treatise by Dr. Gary S. Greig, former Associate Professor of Old Testament and Hebrew, Regent University School of Divinity. He biblically answers questions about angels and many other issues of the Lakeland Outpouring. It is a remarkable piece of work, done at depth. Please check it out. It goes a long, long way to clearing up many misconceptions. http://storage.ignitedchurch.com/drgreg.pdf.

Now, about angels.

Who impregnated Mary? Was it the angel? Or was it the Holy Spirit? Who overshadowed Mary? The Holy Spirit did, right? But who appeared to Mary? The angel did. The angel said, "Mary, the Holy Spirit is about to overshadow you and you will be given a son."

Who is exalted in this situation? Is it the Holy Spirit, or is it the angel? The Holy Spirit, of course!

So why do we get so upset when an angel of the Lord appears and says, "There is a healing outpouring coming now"? It makes no sense. Why are we upset that an angel appears in a room? You have heard various speakers in the Outpouring say, "There's a person right there about to be healed. There is an angel standing right behind them." Why does that upset us? It is not the angel doing the healing. It is an angel pointing to this person, saying, "Hey! This one is going to be healed right now!"

Is our faith so small that we cannot perceive that Holy Spirit can do this? To be upset that angels actually give you information that helps build somebody's faith? If an angel came to you and said, "Joe, two guys are going to walk through that door in just two minutes. I want you to go with them. They going to be a blessing to your life." All of a sudden, two men walk through that door and say, "Are you Joe?" Yes. "Come with us now." There is no explanation, but because the angel has just told you to go ahead and trust, you would get up and go with them. They take you outside and hand you the keys to a brand new hybrid car that gets 50 miles to the gallon! And the title, free and clear...

Why *can't* an angel do that? Why *can't* an angel heal?

Do angels have power to heal the sick? Technically, no. Not any more than a human would. But yes. They've been in the Presence of God. They are a created being. They are an expression of God, ascending and descending from Heaven.

So when an angel touches you, are they touching you with their individual power or are they touching you with the Power of God? It is a matter of semantics. Yes, an angel does have the Power of God on it, or in it, or flowing through it, as a human being does. *How else could an angel minister to you if it doesn't have a way to minister to you?!*

From that standpoint, if an angel touches you, or if an angel stirs the waters, who is doing the healing? Is the angel healing? Or is God healing? It is God healing! But it is the angel that stirred the waters.

Critics are upset about this, because they think that angels can't heal anybody. That's like saying that man can't heal anybody. We can, because it is Christ in us. Because God has given us power to heal the sick. The Bible says, "These signs shall follow them that believe. In My Name, they shall cast out devils." So who has cast out the devil? You did. You released the authority. The spirit of the prophet is subject to the prophet. So, therefore, you are the one who cast out the devil. But you did it in the Name of Jesus.

Let me put it in an even more practical way. Felix is my personal assistant. If I ask, "Felix, I'm in a bind for time. Will you please go to the dry cleaners and get my dry cleaning?" Who goes for the dry cleaning? Is it me, or is it Felix? See, Felix went, but he went in my name. But who picked up the clothes? Felix did. It is a matter of semantics, and it is a matter of understanding.

If, however, Felix goes to pick up my clothes without my permission, he's doing something illegal. That's why you have to be careful—that's where you get into heresy—if somebody tries to use the power of Gifts for their own pursuits, or for their own agenda—at that point, they are in danger of abuse of the Gifts. If I use the Gifts to influence somebody for my benefit, for example if I prophesy that you are going to give $10,000 to my ministry, that is when you are in *dangerous* territory. That happens, frequently. More than anybody would admit.

Here is another problem for the critics. We have asked angels to bring in money. Think about it. How many people on this planet have said, "Lord, would you send your angels to protect me as I travel? Protect this airplane as I fly. Protect my car as I drive." How many times have we done that? Why can you ask an angel to protect you, but you can't ask an angel to bring you resources when you need them?

Chapter Fourteen
Taking the Blessings Home

Impartation is where you come to experience the Presence of God and the Anointing that is at that particular outpouring, and then you take it home and share it at your church. That is the whole concept of coming, getting an impartation, and taking it home. One of the manifestations of an outpouring is that it is *contagious*.

In the last fifty years there has been a measure of impartation in every move of God there has been. In the Charismatic movement, people would come to a meeting and become baptized in the Holy Spirit. Then they'd go back to their church or prayer group to share it. People had prayer groups at their houses and would invite their friends to receive the baptism of the Holy Spirit. Large groups of people were baptized in the Holy Spirit in those home groups. A classic example is Bishop Clarice Fluitt. Probably 10,000 people were baptized in the Holy Spirit—*in her home*, from 1971 to 1974.

The 1993 outpouring with Rodney Howard-Browne was huge. People would come, and sit in one, two, three services and maybe not feel a thing. But then, the next Sunday they'd go back to their church—especially if they were the pastor—and they'd stand up in the pulpit, and the Power of God would hit their church. There are thousands of testimonies of that happening.

I personally experienced that. I would go out to speak after the 1993 Lakeland Outpouring, and I'd just tell stories of what was happening. Spontaneous joy would hit the congregation—without my saying anything about it. Spontaneous joy was the key manifestation of the Lakeland Outpouring in 1993.

It happened to me again this summer in the Philippines. The congregation was weeping; there was a lot of sorrow, a lot of repentance. The Holy Spirit spoke to me and said, "These people have lost their joy."

So I said, "Okay, people. I want you to put your hands up towards heaven. The Holy Spirit just told me he wants to release joy into this house. So, in the Name of Jesus, be filled with joy!"

And I waited. About 30 seconds later, I said, "In the Name of Jesus, be filled with joy." About 30 seconds after that, I said again, "I *said*, in the Name of Jesus, be filled with joy!"

Within three minutes the entire group of 300 people was hit with spontaneous joy. Nothing funny said. No hands laid on anybody. Without any music. Without any prompting from me, except the command to be filled with joy. In the natural, it would be difficult to make someone laugh just by commanding them to do so three times. That is not going to happen, unless you do some kind of antics or are being silly or goofy. But it happened, in the Philippines, this summer.

What is different about this Outpouring? Is it that it is global? No, the Toronto Blessing went global. The Brownsville Revival went global. They were all impartations.

What was different about this Outpouring is that it happened so fast. Within the first twenty days of this Outpouring, we were instantly global. Within the first 30 days, the crowds hit 8,000 or 9,000—*a day*—and climbed to 10,000 people on the weekends. And the global touch from God-TV and the web cast has made it an historic precedent. Nothing has ever happened like this, ever, not this fast.

There have been other outpourings that have had a greater impact, but they lasted longer. The Wales Revival impacted an entire nation. But that was over a three to five year period of time. Toronto lasted three years. Brownsville lasted three years. This Outpouring had as significant an impact internationally in 90 days as other outpourings that went on three or four or five years. The national and international leaders that have been impacted by this in such a short amount of time have been unprecedented. Just to have that many apostles on the platform the night of the Apostolic Alignment was unmatched.

The other unique thing about this Outpouring is that people have experienced impartation over the internet and over the television. That has been significantly greater than anything else before. The prior outpourings that were videotaped went around the world, but they created more of a hunger and a passion. In this Outpouring people have actually been receiving full-blown impartation through the television and the web cast—people grabbing their computer screens or their televisions and being healed! That's happened before, but never like this. We're talking thousands of people healed and or receiving impartation by touching their screen. I even had several people hit by the Power of God because I text messaged them! Many were healed or received impartation through the emails we sent out!

People were writing us daily with all kinds of praise reports. For example, my good friend, Apostle Ormel Chapin, testified that he has seen more miracles, signs and wonders in his ministry after his visit to the Outpouring than at any time in his 25 years of ministry.

Missionary Stephen Kennedy emailed me from Jakarta Indonesia after attending several services in Lakeland:

> We have been going to the Leprosy Colony for about three years now, with a few healings from time to time, but nothing like the last two months Praise God! We have had as many as 80 patients, but now many have gone home!

Freddie and Ann Hayler emailed me:

> Oh, Glory to God...I have watched it and/or been in it every night since day two—my entire life has been changed, my entire ministry has been changed, everything I think has been changed!

> I loved the Lord before with all my heart but the level of faith has gone way up, the ability to know that supernatural experiences are the NORMAL Christian life, and the equipping and teaching gift that has been imparted in these four months has been life-changing!

> Many, many ministries have been birthed from these four months and perhaps this will be similar to the great student missionary movement that catapulted thousands of young people into the mission field. I believe this outpouring has catapulted thousands of young people into the nations worldwide for the last great outpouring and ingathering.

Maria emailed me her testimony. Note how the healing came through a text & voice message:

> On 4/23 while watching God TV via the internet, Todd called out that someone with a bone spur is being healed. I text messaged my husband and also left a voicemail on his cell phone. My husband had been suffering from a bone spur on his foot for the last couple years and doctors could not help him with any correction. My husband was in Detroit, Michigan, for work (our home is in Kansas City). The next day he received my messages and checked his foot and he did not feel any more pain. This last week he mentioned again that he is healed and does not feel any pain. PRAISE GOD!!!!! THANK YOU VERY MUCH!!!

Claudia emailed be from Ohio:

> We just finished spending one week with all of you in Lakeland, Florida, and what can you say but God is doing it!!! We returned to church today in Cincinnati, and did what you told us to do -- we took the impartation home!

> During the service there was a young man wanting to get water baptized. When he came out of the water and started praising God, the *CHILDREN* started asking their moms if they could get baptized also. The first one was my 5-year-old granddaughter. She got in with her clothes on! The pastor asked her why she wanted to do this and she said she loved Jesus with all her heart. Then, at least 15 to 20 others started getting in -- mostly children, and the Fire fell just like when we were in Florida!

> Nothing will stop this fire. This fire in Florida is spreading like wild fire. Children were getting full and changed today, crying and dancing and praising God! It was truly miraculous.

Pastor Alan Koch emailed me:

> I pastor Christ Triumphant Church, a church in an eastern suburb of Kansas City... the "eastern gate" of Kansas City. Most of our staff and I were at the revival for 4 days. There was a release of "fire" when we returned home.

This Sunday was the first one since returning home and the service got "messed up"... we ended up having a fire line... The power of God fell and people were ministered to and healed. We had a guest speaker scheduled and when he EVENTUALLY did get up to speak, the first thing he announced was that his knee was healed without anyone laying hands on it.

This is a transferable anointing! Keep going for it! So are we!

And thousands of praise reports came in *after* people got home. They would email their stories. Marie from Georgia emailed me:

We just wanted to share God's awesome miracle. We live in Georgia and have been watching the Outpouring for the past few weeks. Our 10-year-old daughter, Krystal, was diagnosed with whooping cough on the 24th of April. She was on 1000mg of antibiotics, she had received 2 steroid shots, and she was on a nebulizer. Nothing was working.

On May 1st, we made a declaration that we were coming to Lakeland for her healing! As soon as we made that decision, she took a turn for the worse (fever, loss of voice) and our van broke down. We realized the devil was trying to stop us! We got our van fixed (a $600 problem), picked it up from the mechanic on Saturday morning and were headed to Lakeland by 4pm.

As we got closer, Krystal called to us from the back of the van. We were so excited to hear her voice (it had been over a week since she had been able to talk). We were not sure if we would be able to get in to the Outpouring because there was no parking! We found (made) one!

When we got inside, we found seats in the bleachers. We all laid hands on Krystal and felt her buckle under the Power in the stadium. We told her to cough, but nothing came out!!! (Whooping cough sounds like a seal barking--just worse). We were so excited. My husband, Kenneth, ran down to the testimony line with her. The power of God was so strong, she fell to her knees. My husband had to put her on his back and carry her back to the bleachers.

My in-laws had seen Krystal earlier that day and were really worried. We drove the two hours back to their home after the service. They were in awe. God is soooooo good. We thank Him for her healing; we thank Him for being debt free.

Not praying during impartation?

One critic put on his website that I told pastors to stop praying during impartation. He obviously didn't hear me correctly.

I often explain to the pastors that we as Pentecostals have a serious problem with talking too much. Even Jesus said, "When you pray, stop repeating your prayers, thinking you are going to be heard because of your much speaking." How many times have you been to a Pentecostal prayer meeting and it's, "Hallelujah, Halleloooooooojah, Hallelu-yia, Jesus, Jesus, Jesus, Jesus...." We talk and talk and talk and talk. We are just as repetitive with our prayers as Catholics who repeat ten Our Fathers and twenty Hail Mary's. There is no difference. We talk too much when we pray.

How rude would it be if I were to ask you a question and then start answering the question for you, or simply to keep asking the same question over and over again without giving you a space to answer? Yet, we do that with God. Lord, forgive me of my sin. Then, why aren't we quiet for a moment to let Him tell us about the sins He is concerned about?

So, for impartation, I told the pastors, I want you to spend the next few minutes while you are waiting for me to come to you in the line, make sure that everything is right between you and God, and everything is right between you and man. That is what you are to do while you are standing here. You're asking God to cleanse you of all sin. Then you tell God that you forgive anyone who has ever hurt you or harmed you, and then you release them. Get rid of unforgiveness and bitterness in your heart, and make a commitment to the Lord that, if possible, you will go to the person who has offended you, or a person you have offended, and make things right. Write an email, write a letter, make a phone call, make a personal visit — do something to make it right. Maybe the person has died or moved away and you have no idea where they are or even who it was...but, if possible, make it right. While you are waiting in the prayer line, get straight.

Then, I go on to tell them, some of you will physically feel the Touch of the Lord during impartation. But most of you won't. For me, personally, probably 70% of the time I feel nothing physically when the anointing is in the room. I often tell people, you can't go by feelings. It is a receiving by faith.

That is what the whole Christian experience is—receiving by faith.

But, once I lay hands on you, stop talking. The moment the mantle of God touches you, or releases healing, or releases impartation into the atmosphere, shut up and receive it, by faith. Even say, "I receive," and then just pause, capturing the moment, consciously receiving whatever impartation God has for you. Be still. Be still. Be still....and receive... And then *respond!!!*

Chapter Fifteen
The Apostolic Alignment

The astounding amount of controversy admittedly caught me off guard. I had no idea how apparently prejudiced the Christian world was to Todd's ministry. I never found anything in his ministry that concerned me. Even his tattoos didn't bother me. Frankly, I had to work through being offended by some of my ministry friends who were expressing their "concerns" publicly. Some were writing in their emails, blogs, magazines or newsletters. Others actually preached sermons about their concerns. I would receive audio recordings from the "heresy hunters" saying, "Even his friends are speaking against him."

And, now that it has been revealed that Todd Bentley has serious character flaws, these same critics are saying, "I told you so," causing even more harm and pain. Interestingly, 95% of their concerns were with their understanding of his doctrine, not his character faults. The few who expressed concerns about his character did so for something that happened when he was twelve years old!

The thing that hurt was that these ministry friends had my cell phone number and email address and never tried to contact me. Most still have not. Even when I tried to reach out to ask why they hadn't contacted me, it was like they had a blind-spot to what they had done. Never apologized; simply said they felt they had to "express themselves" because so many of their constituents were "asking them" for answers.

Admittedly, I've needed a lot of prayer and counseling to keep my spirit pure of offense. I've also had to apologize to some for my "rebukes." I literally had to work my way through repentance daily. One of the side effects of this Outpouring has been a work of holiness and the fear of God. I can't go for more than a few minutes in any kind of sin before I feel God's hand squeezing me! Temptation of any kind is met with a swift move of the Spirit – followed by strong repentance. That's one of the reasons why I know beyond any shadow of a doubt – this is God!

For some reason, the Body of Christ seems to have ignored the scriptures that admonish us to "hear both sides of the story." Even the secular press would at least call us for a "comment" before writing a story about the Outpouring. Yet our Christian brothers never once tried to contact us. They appear to have ignored the scriptures that tell us to "go to our brother who we feel is overtaken in a fault." Instead, they have used the "bully pulpit" of their emails, newsletters, and websites to express "their concerns" that often – so far – in my opinion, have been based on incomplete or misinformation.

A few friends and I were able to put together "statements" and "theological responses" to some of the "concerns," but even these responses were ignored or refused.[35] It appeared to me that many simply are predisposed to feel that this outpouring was demonic, period. It's like trying to convince a non-Pentecostal that speaking in tongues is really for today. No matter what scripture you give them, they have chosen NOT to believe.

And to those who labeled this as a work of an angel of light or a deceiving spirit or familiar spirit – do they know what they were saying? Isn't it a sin to attribute the work of the Holy Spirit to Satan? How could we worship for up to two hours per service, preach the Gospel, exalt Christ, preach holiness—and be operating in a demonic spirit? I was baffled by their assessments.

My prayer for the Body of Christ is that we learn that "eye has not seen, nor ear heard, what God has in store for us..." So that when we "see" something new, we truly investigate it from all sides before we label it "not of God." Is it possible that God is doing something "new?"

All I know for sure is that I love Jesus more than I've ever loved Him before. I can't even write these few words without tears flowing from my eyes. People were saved in the meetings and in the marketplace. Many in the Body of Christ appeared to have a renewed faith in miracles, and we got dozens of requests daily for the dead to be raised. Over thirty recorded resurrections or "come back to life" stories have been received since we began. Multiple funerals were cancelled. I'd say that was pretty good verification.

---

35 Please see Dr. Gary S. Greig's "**A Theological Response to Criticism of the Lakeland Outpouring and Todd Bentley:** *BIBLICAL REASONS TO RECEIVE GOD'S GLORY AND GIVE IT AWAY IN POWER EVANGELISM* at http://storage.ignitedchurch.com/drgreg.pdf. His scriptural analysis will aid you in deciding for yourself what is right and wrong.

At one point I had over 5,000 praise reports on my computer that I hadn't been able to read! Fresh Fire and God-TV also had too many to count! What will it take for us even to "suggest" that maybe, just maybe, God was doing something fresh?

The Apostolic Alignment

Around the end of May, I called Peter Wagner, who is the president and founder of International Coalition of Apostles. "Peter, where are the apostles?" I asked. "Todd and I are sitting here, totally being shot at from all sides. The "heresy hunters" are crucifying us. The "revival police" are screaming.

"Where are the apostles? You have taught me that the apostles need to rise up and take their place. For the past ten years we've been talking about the restoration of apostles. This is day sixty of the Outpouring and I have not heard from the apostles. Instead, my apostle buddies are saying things, writing things in Christian magazines, preaching sermons from their pulpits. The "heresy hunters" are sending the apostles' concerns to me, instead of my getting it directly from my friends. Not one leader in the International Coalition of Apostles, of which I am a dues-paying member, has called me."

I was, as you might discern, getting it off my chest. Peter simply said, "Let me make some phone calls."

Before Peter hung up, he wanted to know who Todd's apostles were. I told Peter that I thought he had some kind of relationship with Che Ahn, John Arnott, and Bill Johnson.

"Ah," he said, "Che Ahn is perfect. I consider him a son. I'll call Che Ahn."

What Peter had in mind was an Apostolic Alignment, a ceremony that would put Todd in a formal relationship with the Revival Alliance. We felt it imperative to stand with the apostles, and have the Alignment—so we could be certain our Biblical backbone was straight.

The only day that all three of them had free that would possibly work was June 23. Monday night. The *only* day! I was in the middle of the Philippines, preaching. I had to change my flights and cut my stay in half to come home. I got back Monday morning after a 35-hour flight and never even went to bed.

Both Che Ahn and John Arnott had to return from overseas or come across country, too. We arrived just in time for the service. Actually, Che Ahn arrived in the service late because the engine fell off of his plane! Fortunately, it was on the ground at the time. But they had to change to a new plane, and it took an inordinate amount of extra time.

The platform was a beehive of activity. We had no idea whether or not Che would be able to make it in time. Everything hinged on his being there. We had messages going back and forth continually. Che is stuck in Ohio. Che is still an hour away. We were continually getting new information, which was then distributed to the leaders on the platform. We discussed worst case scenarios: what do we do if Che can't get here? Up until 9:00 p.m., we didn't even know whether Che was on the ground.

He actually walked in at 10:15 or 10:20—which was the absolute last five-minute window we had to start the Apostolic Alignment. As it was, we went 15 minutes over our deadline. Fortunately, God-TV gave us an extra 15 minutes because of Che's being late. What if God-TV had not been able to give us that extra 15 minutes? The world would have missed all of the prophetic words. But the Holy Spirit had it well in hand.

Che Ahn, John Arnott and Bill Johnson formed a semicircle behind Peter Wagner and Todd. Members of the International Coalition of Apostles and other apostles—who had been in the meetings, and who had been able to get there on such short notice—circled around, too. Bishop Clarice Fluitt was there. International apostles, including Jeff Beacham from Australia, Sharon Stone from England, Paco Garcia from Spain, Barry Boucher and Wesley Campbell, both from Canada, joined American leaders Rick Joyner of South Carolina, Michael and Richard Maiden from Arizona, Joshua Fowler from Orlando, and Doris Wagner from Colorado. And, blessing of blessing, my Dad and I stood shoulder to shoulder, directly behind Peter Wagner. *All on camera. Live around the world.*

Peter read a document about the apostolic alignment. He turned to Todd and asked, "Todd, do you recognize these three men as your apostolic accountability? Todd said, "I do." Peter turned to the three apostles and asked, "Do you receive Todd into the Revival Alliance?" And they said "I do."

Che Ahn, Bill Johnson, and John Arnott laid hands on Todd and anointed him with oil. Todd went down under the Power, lying on the platform. The apostles knelt and prayed.

Then Che Ahn asked all of the apostles, "Does anyone have a Word?" About six of them had powerful prophetic words, either directly for Todd or into the ceremony. But right in the middle of the Words, Bishop Clarice Fluitt gave a prophetic declaration. When she finished, the place erupted. It just exploded! I'll tell you about that in a moment.

All this went on from about 10:20 to 11:15 p.m. At the end they brought up all of the Fresh Fire associates and interns, and the Revival Alliance laid hands on all of them. Next, they brought up all of the apostles, and the Revival Alliance prayed for them. The stage was in utter holy chaos until midnight. As we left the platform, Fresh Fire associates and interns created a giant fire tunnel and prayed for everybody in the place. This went until 12:30 a.m.

This all happened on Monday night, June 23, 2008. Remember the date. It was an historic event. Here is what I believe happened in Spirit.

First of all, Todd was brought into total alignment before the whole world as being under apostolic authority and full support. The Revival Alliance is now globally recognized as his apostolic authority. We established that Todd was responsible in mutual submission to the Revival Alliance. So what does that mean? That means if Todd began to do something questionable, the Revival Alliance would be responsible to bring him into line.

And now, as the world has learned, Todd does have some serious flaws, and the Revival Alliance immediately picked up their responsibilities and began their process of correction and restoration. It is my personal conviction that God was waiting for this alignment to take place so he could bring correction into Todd's life. It was the apostles who exposed Todd's sin, NOT the media.

But beyond that, that night when Bishop Clarice Fluitt prophesied, at that exact moment, I believe that *full restoration of the apostolic was set in place*. This is what she said to Todd—and to the world—

> For the word of the Lord would say, 'Behold a vanguard. Behold the tugboat that is cutting through the ice of religious traditions--the cruel, hard things. The understanding of the mind of man will now bow to the reality of the revelation of the finished work of Calvary.
>
> Behold, saith God, you have been equipped with cutting power. You have been equipped to go through those traditions of the mind of man, saith God, and you are pulling the church into the realm of glory. Behind you is a great ship that is laden with healing, deliverance, and prosperity.
>
> This is the word to you, O man of God: Arise, kill and eat.
>
> **No longer, no longer, no longer will men call unclean what I have called clean.**

Do not call unclean what I have declared to be clean. Arise, son of man, kill and eat.

When Bishop Clarice spoke these Scriptural words into the ceremony, I believe that the restoration of the entire apostolic movement was complete. It had come into its fullness.

The room exploded. The people weren't applauding her. They were responding to the authority that was released into the heavens when she said her final words.

When she said that and the crowd exploded, my spirit man was so impacted, my body literally doubled over, although I didn't feel anything physically. It responded as though I had been punched in the belly; I had to hold onto my Dad to keep from going over. Many in the audience had a similar experience of impact. It was like an atomic bomb had gone off. Then it was over, in seconds.

In a nutshell, we've been preaching for the last 25 years the restoration of the evangelist, restoration of the pastor, restoration of the prophet, the restoration of the teacher. The last is the apostle. And when the last restoration of the five-fold ministry is in effect, then a new glory will be released. I believe, without a shadow of a doubt, that when Bishop Fluitt spoke those words, the restoration of the apostle took place, snap, at that second.

When I asked Bishop Clarice what she felt the Holy Spirit meant when He apparently declared Todd "clean" when we now know he wasn't, she indicated that it was the "work of the Holy Spirit *through* Todd that was clean, not necessarily the vessel."

Rick Joyner

I received an article from Rick Joyner that I think is a masterpiece. It was done as an evaluation of the commissioning, of the revival, and Todd Bentley. It is objective, and unbelievably Christian in its approach. It should be a pattern to follow for the future in evaluating someone's ministry.

An interesting note is that Rick Joyner is now playing a strategic role in Todd's restoration.

"The Ordination"
By Rick Joyner

This past Monday I was invited to the Lakeland Revival to be present at Todd Bentley's ordination. For the sake of clarity, this was not Todd's ordination into ministry, which he received long ago, but was a specific ordination by a small group including Bill Johnson, Che Ahn, and John Arnott. These three have agreed to help oversee Todd's ministry for the "Lakeland Revival." It was a unique and specific type of ordination that I think the Lord was in. I was asked to be there with some others who represent different streams that appreciate and support what is happening in Lakeland and Todd's ministry in particular. I also wanted to be there to express the high degree of trust and appreciation for the three who have agreed to oversee Todd's ministry in this way.

The Lakeland Revival is now a world event, touching many nations and denominations. As its impact has grown, so has the controversy and persecution. That is standard for any true move of God, and we should not be surprised by it. This is especially true of ministries or movements that release God's power for healing, miracles, and deliverance. When the Lord Jesus started performing miracles, the persecution began in earnest. When the miracles became more spectacular, the persecution increased. When He raised someone from the dead, the conservative religious community of the times resolved to kill Him. That startling hardness of heart is the result of letting a religious spirit gain dominion in our lives. *A main strategy of the religious spirit is to get us to honor what God has done in order to justify persecuting what He is doing.*

I have known Todd Bentley for about a decade, and he is a man of exceptional theological depth, revelatory gifting, and the leader of a large and growing multi-faceted ministry that has had a significant impact on many nations. I have been to Abbotsford, B.C. a few times to speak at Fresh Fire Conferences, and I always marvel at the substance and excellence of what Todd has been able to build in such a short period of time as well as the quality of people on his team.

I am saying all of this because there is much more to Todd Bentley and Fresh Fire Ministries than has yet been revealed through what is now happening in Lakeland. I know Todd as someone who can teach or preach with a rare depth and clarity, but Lakeland is not really about that, at least not yet. It is about an impartation of faith, power, and fire. Right now we, the body of Christ, need these more than we need more teaching and strategy.

One of the basic laws of physics applies here. You cannot change the direction of an object unless it is moving, and before we need more strategy and direction, we need to wake up the church and get it moving. Lakeland is waking up the church, including the many who are naysayers and critics, but at least she is being awakened.

Now I do not want to dismiss all of the naysayers or critics too quickly. They serve their purpose and can be very helpful, even if not in the way that they presume. This is not to say that Todd or the Lakeland Revival cannot make mistakes. None of us is perfect. However, if someone is going to criticize, we need to check their credentials. If someone has a significant healing and miracle ministry, we should listen to them in relation to the ministry of healing and miracles. If someone has been used to start and shepherd a significant revival, I would listen to him much more about his views of a revival than someone who has only read or written about them.

A Chord of Three Strands

Now let's look briefly at the credentials of the three who have agreed to oversee Todd's ministry in the Lakeland Revival. John Arnott was used by God to start and oversee the extraordinary Toronto Renewal. This is a move of God that has touched and helped heal and renew multitudes of believers, churches, and even whole movements and denominations, around the world. It is also a fire that has continued to burn for over a decade — a remarkable accomplishment in the history of revivals and renewal movements. With this kind of experience, it makes him a true elder in the church in the gate of renewal or revival movements.

Bill Johnson not only has a significant healing and miracle ministry, but he is one of the greatest equippers who has been used to help release and mature these gifts in thousands of students who have come through his school in Redding, California, as well as stirring them up in a large part of the body of Christ through his books, teachings, and travels. Bill has done this from and through the local church setting, seeking to release these gifts in a major way to and through the church. Throughout much of the advancing church at this time, Bill Johnson would be in just about everyone's top few of authorities on healing, miracles, and understanding the supernatural aspects of the Christian walk.

Che Ahn is one of the emerging great church builders. He is not only the leader of a significant church in Pasadena, but Harvest International Ministries is now a network of hundreds of churches. He is a church man who loves the church, and his heartbeat message is about building the church with a kingdom perspective. Lou Engle, the leader of The Call, one of the most powerful ministries mobilizing the youth and intercessory prayer in our times, was raised up under Che Ahn. When they called together youth to the mall in Washington a few years ago, more than 400,000 responded. On August 16, The Call in Washington could gather even more. Che Ahn knows how to build healthy local churches, to raise up and release new movements, as well as how to help oversee huge gatherings of God's people for important events.

Personal Observations from Lakeland

I was only in Lakeland for a few hours and had to leave the meeting right after the ordination. I also try to keep in mind that "we see in part." Even so, the following is a little more from a personal perspective about what is happening in Lakeland.

When I first heard about the outbreak in Lakeland, I felt that it was the beginning of something very significant and maybe the beginning of what we have been waiting for. When I first watched some of it on God-TV, I became even more excited. After being there for just a few minutes, I was even more so. This is a major impartation from God, and it will have significant consequences for what is about to unfold.

I wanted to go to the tent before many people did so I could get a feel for the place, but there were already thousands worshiping, praying, and fellowshipping there long before the meeting was to start. The place was charged with expectation. I saw many people I knew, and everyone I saw seemed more alive than the last time I'd seen them, even people from our own congregation at Heritage. I took a seat on the second row to kind of absorb the atmosphere. The quickening was so strong that I decided if nothing happened from the platform, it was well worth coming to just sit in that quickening atmosphere.

They came to get me to sit on the platform, and it was interesting how the anointing seemed different there. It was still good, but different. Even so, I enjoyed seeing Todd and a number of other friends I had not seen in awhile. When Todd came over and put his arm around me, it was a hug, but I also felt that I kind of needed to hold him up. He is under the kind of anointing that does stagger you and actually makes you feel drunk, which is why they thought the disciples on the Day of Pentecost were drunk with wine. Under this kind of anointing, I knew Todd might not be able to do some of the in-depth teaching and preaching he is capable of, but I don't think that is really the purpose of Lakeland anyway.

Probably the greatest revival in church history was The Welsh Revival of 1904 – 1906, and there was no significant message that came out of it other than God moving and awakening His church, which it did around the world. The Azusa Street Revival was different—it was about the baptism in the Holy Spirit. Even though the main theme of Lakeland seems to be the healing and miracles, I think it may actually be about something more, but more subtle.

In studying Azusa Street and the writings that came out of the early leaders of the Pentecostal Movement, I occasionally happened upon a remarkable belief that many of them had. They were convinced that what they had received was the true baptism in the Holy Spirit, but many were still looking for another baptism to come—the baptism of fire. As is typical of this type of thing, even with the baptism in the Holy Spirit before it came, there was not much definition given to what they thought the baptism of the Holy Spirit and fire would be like. Many were expecting another element (the fire aspect) of the baptism, but I never read where any thought that they had received this aspect.

Of course, the theology of this is debatable, but I have expected a baptism of fire to come upon the church that would so consume the Laodicean lukewarmness that the church would be radically transformed by it. I have prophesied it in a number of ways which has been sown throughout my writings and messages, mostly as a great passion for the Lord. I saw that this passion for Jesus would be so contagious that anyone who got close to it would be infected, and once infected could never be cured! It was a fiery love for the Son of God that would come upon the church so that she would truly do everything she needed to do to be a worthy bride prepared for the coming King. This fire would also make His messengers like flames of fire burning with passion for His gospel and His purposes.

I know that Lakeland is mostly about healing and miracles,

which are crucial aspects of the Lord's ministry that are being reawakened in the church and imparted to many there. Even so, I felt fire when I was there. I am not yet saying this is it, but I think one thing that is being released there is at least a preparation for a coming baptism of fire upon the church. We may not be able to give the true definition of this until it has come. At the very least, those who come to Lakeland with an open heart will leave with a renewed fire in their heart for the Lord.

The Lakeland Outpouring has already become a major infusion of zeal for the Lord that is impacting a large part of the church in a very positive way. For too many years, almost every Christian leader was saying "the Lord is about to do something." Now almost everyone I talk to is saying "the Lord is doing something!" Where there has been hope, it has jumped into faith and expectation, and where the Lord finds this He will do wonders.

Todd has an amazing depth, maturity, and wisdom for his age, but he is still young. He might say some things wrong occasionally and say or do things that are hard to understand. His tattoos are real hard for some people to take, but those tattoos seem to be the very thing that have attracted many, especially the emerging generation, to him and his message. I have heard numerous reports of people who have become almost addicted to watching the revival on God-TV because they were channel surfing and were so captivated by Todd's appearance that they could not stop watching. Then they started listening. Now they are on fire for God.

Even those who would never get a tattoo at least view him as a genuine person with no facades. My opinion of Todd for the years I have known him is that he is one of the most genuine people I have ever known, still untainted by religion, but one of the greatest lovers of God and His truth. He is also deeply compassionate, and is greatly touched by people's infirmities, which is always the foundation of a true healing ministry. Todd is the real thing, and he has many very real people around him who are true friends of God.

As stated, that does not mean Todd could never stumble or make mistakes. He could just like any of us. I think Todd is a lot like the Peter, who would either walk on water or drown trying. He will press the limits, and like Peter, be used for some of the greatest breakthroughs, but at times need a severe rebuke. People with that nature do make mistakes, but they are also the ones who do the greatest exploits, and it is obvious that the Lord really loves people like Peter. If Peter had not been there on the Day of Pentecost, there probably would not have been a harvest of three thousand souls, but maybe only twenty.

Todd has been sent to offend the religious spirit and to be an offense to the complacent, and thank the Lord it is working. Todd came to Concord, North Carolina last week to do a one-night meeting. The arena was packed to overflowing with eight thousand people, and reports were that there were as many turned away as who got in. There was gridlock on Hwy 49 for over six miles. When the police drove up and down the road, telling people to go home because no more could get into the arena, crowds poured out of their cars just to worship on the side of the road. That sounds like true revival to me.

Usually your greatest strengths can also be your greatest weaknesses, and Todd is vulnerable. Everyone has blind sides, and though I appreciate Todd seeking covering from those he thinks can help him stay on track, no amount of human covering can keep us from making mistakes. It is also hard to be on stage every night for as long as he is and not occasionally say or do something wrong or foolish.

If Todd does something foolish, it will probably be in front of an international television audience. He has many critics that are waiting like packs of wolves to jump on anything they can. The more that power is released, the more vicious these attacks will become. We really need to discern between the voice of the true shepherds and the voice of the accuser of the brethren, who will use any inroad he can to get brethren to accuse other brethren. Historically, the most vicious of all attacks have come from threatened church leaders, especially the leaders of the previous move of God. This is a terrible tragedy that we really need to pray will get broken this time."

-- Rick Joyner

The Passing of the Baton

It was shortly after the Apostolic Alignment that Todd began to speak less and less at the tent. At first we were told by his staff that he was exhausted and needed to rest. I requested to meet with him just to encourage him. But it just never worked out. As a matter of fact, the last full conversation that I had with Todd was two weeks before the alignment ceremony.

Fresh Fire staff began to let me know that Todd felt that he needed to take the outpouring around the world and that he would probably want to pass the baton to me soon. We finally set a date for August 23. I felt in my spirit that it would actually happen before that and got my key staff ready in case it happened sooner.

Soon the news came to me that Todd's marriage was shaky and that his wife was going back to Canada for rest and counseling. Again I tried to meet with Todd, but was told he was too emotional about the whole thing and really wasn't seeing anyone. One night, I came to the tent for the service and security ushered me to Todd's trailer behind the tent. I had never been invited in there before a service. The Fresh Fire staff informed me that Todd was too upset to speak and that I would be preaching. I went over and sat down beside him and I just told him I loved him and I was happy to do it. So I left the room after about three minutes and went to the platform and preached.

A few days later, the Fresh Fire staff informed me that Todd had decided to close the tent and move back to Ignited Church on August 3. I thought that was a great idea because it would mean that God TV would be broadcasting from our church for the last three weeks, and this would encourage people to continue coming to Ignited long after that August 23 date when Todd had announced he would be leaving Lakeland and heading across Europe.

On Wednesday, August 6th, Todd was scheduled to preach at Ignited. I was resting in my office before the service and Todd asked to see me. We sat for a few minutes and he told me that his marriage difficulties were really getting to him emotionally. I assured him of our love and support. He told me that he wanted to get into the worship as soon as possible so he could just be refreshed in God's presence. So we headed to the platform. The service had just started. I walked up on the stage but noticed he didn't follow me. About thirty minutes later, security told me Todd wanted to see me. I went back stage and joined a huddle with his staff and God TV. Todd informed me that he was going to pass the baton of the outpouring to me immediately and that I would be preaching.

I felt at perfect peace about everything, but I just insisted that he at least tell the outpouring story because so many people were now watching live on God TV, and many had never heard how it started in our church. He was very reluctant and didn't feel he could do it without my help. He didn't want to break down in front of the TV audience as had happened to him in England. I told him I would stand by his side. Together, we went onto the platform where Todd and I dialogued back and forth, telling the story of how the Outpouring came to be.

Todd called my wife, Janice, to the platform. He laid hands on Janice and me, and passed the baton to us and Ignited Church. Then I called up my pastors and elders and we laid hands on Todd and sent him to the nations with the Outpouring. I took over the service and that is the last time I saw or spoke to Todd to this day. It wouldn't be until August 12th that I knew of any of Todd's failures.

About a month later, Todd did text message me and apologized, and I immediately texted him back and assured him of our forgiveness, love, and support.

Chapter Sixteen
More from "That's My Roger" Rhonda!

When I came home from Lakeland the time I prayed for "my Roger," my husband Jim saw such a change in me that he wanted to go and experience...experience what? What do you experience at an outpouring!!? I called my friend Chris to have her look for airline tickets for us.

Now, the last few years have been a real financial challenge. We have real estate to sell. All of our money is tied up in land payments and our house payment. We are real close to running out of money. So when Chris called to tell me that she had found tickets for $410.00 each it might as well have been $4,000.00.

I told her my concern and she said, "You need to know that God wants you there and that it won't be just another trip."

When I told Jim the price, he said, "I believe we are supposed to go," and the cost is what it is.

I went back to pick up the phone and Chris was crying. She said, "I changed the return one day and it dropped it to $177.00." She said, "I know you're supposed to go, I know God wants you there."

YIPPEE...This is a God thing and we were on our way!

Tuesday, July 8, was our first evening meeting. Todd was on the platform during worship, and when that was over he left. We didn't know he wouldn't be returning. He wasn't there any of the other nights we were there. But that was ok. We didn't go there because of Todd. We were there to have an encounter with Jesus. And that we did.

Many asked, "Where is Todd? When is Todd coming back? I came all this way to see Reverend Bentley...Where is he and when is he coming back?"

We would just say, "I know nothing about Todd, but this I do know...Jesus is in the house...He shows up every night. If you came to see Jesus, you won't be disappointed."

One night, someone came to Jim pushing an empty wheel chair. He said, "What do I do with this?" Jim asked, "With what?" The man answered, "This wheel chair. I prayed for the person who was once in it, and they got up and walked away." What a problem—an empty wheel chair.

Then came July 13, our last night at the tent. Jesus showed up and turned the lights off...literally. After worship, someone came up to the podium. I didn't know who he was and didn't care. I came to meet Jesus. As soon as the speaker opened his mouth, I recognized the voice; it was James Goll. What a humble servant... mighty man of God. He prophesied, decreed, declared, prayed, shouted...everything he said resonated with us. Pastor Goll had spent the previous 24 hours alone with God, and he was telling us about his time with God.

Then the lights went out...the men on the platform circled James. Since no one had a clue what was happening I suppose it was to protect him. The only lights on were from the EXIT signs. Someone on the platform got a flashlight and James told him to shine it on his notes. And there, right where he left off speaking, it said, "Either the lights would go off or the fire alarm would." It was electrifying. He told us that God had told him a few years before (I think) that God would connect him with Todd. God said, "You need his raw faith and he needs your wisdom."

Todd wasn't at the tent that week in July, but Jesus was. And it was worth the price we paid...every penny. Would I go again? Oh, yes.

--Rhonda Martens

Chapter Seventeen
A Jesus Explosion from the Epicenter?

Fascinating, just to read deeply the words spoken into the Apostolic Alignment.[36] There are some that might now be interpreted as warnings of the coming "test."

I am not speaking simply of Todd's test, even though he has lost everything he holds most dear—most particularly his ministry for God (at least for a season, however long that may be). He has lost his dignity. And he seemingly has brought disgrace to Christ—or that is what people are saying...screaming.... Screaming, and cursing, and condemning, and hating...all those things that Jesus was trying to teach us *not* to do. Is that how *your* heart reacted?

During the first few weeks of the Outpouring, Rick Joyner answered a series of questions that people were asking. One was: How does one restore a fallen leader, and can a fallen leader return to the pulpit?

This is Rick's cogent answer, a remarkably clear, well-thought, Christ-like piece of wisdom.

> The "how to" of restoring fallen leaders is a question that may have a big impact, not only on the present outpouring, but on all future ones as well. The body of Christ, in general, has not done well in restoring falling leaders in recent times, but we must, as we are told in Galatians 6:1:
>
> *Brethren, even if a man is caught in any trespass, you who are spiritual, restore such a one in a spirit of gentleness; each one looking to yourself, lest you too be tempted.*[37]

---

36 The complete Apostolic Alignment ceremony, including all words spoken in prophecy, may be found in Appendix II in the back of this book.

37 *"Live creatively, friends. If someone falls into sin, forgivingly restore him, saving your critical comments for yourself. You might be needing forgiveness before the day is out. Stoop down and reach out to those who are oppressed. Share their burdens, and so complete Christ's law. If you think you are too good for that, you are badly deceived."* Galatians 6:1 The Message Bible

One "how to" in restoration that we read here is to do it in a spirit of gentleness, looking to ourselves, which I think implies that we could all fall were it not for the grace of God. Keep this in mind or we, too, will be tempted. We should never approach this with the arrogance that we have not fallen, but rather just to help a brother or sister, who is also one of God's own children.

We can also conclude from this verse that the **"spiritual"** do restore others. Restoration, which includes redemption and reconciliation, is the basic purpose of God in the earth, and is therefore a foundation of all true ministry.

We also can conclude from this verse that anyone who has done anything should qualify for restoration. However, restoration means far more than just forgiving them; it means getting them back to where they were before they fell.

It is also obvious that when one has fallen deeply and for a long time into a transgression, the restoration process will almost certainly be deep and lengthy. The restoration for those who fall means their minds must be renewed; a process that can take years for even the most devoted Christians. This is rarely an easy or quick matter.

For example, it would be wrong to treat a single fall to immorality the same way that we would someone who has been in one adulterous affair after another for many years. It is true that even a single adulterous encounter still reveals a gate of hell that is open into someone's life, and it must be found and shut, but it is foolish to treat two entirely different matters like this the same.

Stealing a candy bar is not the same as murder. However, someone who murdered in an instance of jealous rage when doing something like catching a spouse in an affair, may not take as long to restore as someone who has been a petty thief all of his life. We have to take every case individually. I also doubt that there has ever been perfect repentance or perfect restoration.

We are not trying to make people perfect, but whole.

Here is the underlying, crucial phrase from Galatians: *you who are spiritual.* We who are spiritual are required—*required*—to restore others. Are you a Christian, in name only? Or do you believe that we must live in the imitation of Christ—not only in our outer actions, but in our thoughts and in our hearts?

Jesus Christ would have us be compassionate, and surround a fallen brother or sister with intense love, in our prayers and in our hearts.

You see, there is another "test" here in those prophecies spoken into the Apostolic Alignment, and this one is for you and me. It is a glorious Holy Spirit concept. It requires that, for a season, we lay aside our feelings of anger or betrayal or disgust and listen to a new way of thinking.

It will require that we simply take a few moments, get quiet, and ask the Holy Spirit for insight. Then, we simply read and listen, and *measure it by your heart.*

I want to show you again Dr. Sharon Stone's prophecy. Dr. Stone is the British apostle over Christian International Europe. She is now suffering for that prophecy. But, please, look again at what Dr. Stone *actually* said.

> *Todd, the Spirit of God says years from now people will look at this time and they will recognize it as when their God showed up and created within the church a new heart, says the Lord. And I will genesis in the midst of the chaos in the world today and I will not just bring a mending, but I will bring forth that which is new, that which is dedicated, that which is decided, that which is pure.*
>
> *And I will heal the corruptness of the heart, says God, and this is the heart that I will not despise. And as David cried unto me, 'Don't take your Holy Spirit from me,' I have released a cry within my church, says the Lord, that has begun to release its desperation and said, 'I can't live without your presence, I can't live without your glory; I'm undone and I am naked without your presence. No program will be a substitute.' And the Spirit of God says history will measure it by heart.*

Perhaps it doesn't look to the larger Christian community as though the Spirit of God showed up. But those of us who were in those meetings, who actually *felt* that sacred presence, who actually were *healed* of dire illnesses (and even scars), who actually *received* direct communication from the Holy Spirit as to some defect in our own character or some direction God wanted us to take in our own lives—we know differently. There is a new heart in the Body of Christ.

And, after the Apostolic Alignment, which we took in order to be absolutely certain our spiritual backbone was straight, the Spirit of God showed up again, to cleanse our brother and the Outpouring. *"And I will heal the corruptness of the heart, says God, and this is the heart that I will not despise."* **And this is the heart that I will not despise**.

Now, the Spirit of God is showing up again, in the largest context ever. *"I will not just bring a mending, but I will bring forth that which is new, that which is dedicated, that which is decided, that which is pure."* Now it is up to each of us to participate in that mending and bringing forth that which is pure.

We, the Body of Christ—that inclusive, love-filled, transparent, golden corporate man that Bishop Clarice prophesied—have an *unbelievable* opportunity to further the Kingdom of Christ. And as the Body of Christ, we need to unite in the supernatural so we may explode this Outpouring with a flooding of Christ's love—the fireworks at the closing of an outdoors concert—a finale that never ends!

Are you willing?

Appendix I

Apostolic Alignment Ceremony

=====================================
APOSTOLIC ALIGNMENT CEREMONY
=====================================

Dr. Peter Wagner, President of the International Coalition of Apostles

Dr. Wagner invites the following ministers to the platform to stand beside him: Todd Bentley, Che Ahn, Bill Johnson, and John Arnott

Then Dr. Wagner invites the following group of apostles to stand behind him: Stephen Strader, Lakeland, Florida; Karl Strader, Lakeland, Florida; Jeff Beacham, Sydney, Australia; Rick Joyner, Fort Mills, South Carolina; Doris Wagner, Colorado Springs, Colorado; Sharon Stone, Burton, England; Paco Garcia, Checlana, Spain; Bishop Clarice Fluitt, Monroe, Louisiana; Richard Maiden, Scottsdale, Arizona; Mike Maiden, Phoenix, Arizona; Joshua Fowler, Orlando, Florida; Barry Boucher, Ontario, Canada; Wesley Campbell, Calona, Canada.

Personal note: For the sake of historical significance, I'm including the actual document that was read by Dr. Wagner.

===
LAKELAND OUTPOURING APOSTOLIC ALIGNMENT
June 23, 2008
C. Peter Wagner

A warm welcome to those of you who are present in this tent and to you who are watching through GOD TV. You are about to witness an event which could well have historic implications not only for the Lakeland Outpouring but also for our nation and for many other nations of the world. Prophets have been telling us for years that God is about to launch an extraordinary spiritual awakening with signs and wonders, and for over two months Todd Bentley has been leading one of the more obvious fulfillments of those prophecies. This is an exciting place to be right now!

My name is Peter Wagner and I am President of Global Harvest Ministries based in Colorado Springs, Colorado. I have served the body of Christ in apostolic ministry for many years, and currently I preside over the International Coalition of Apostles which brings together over 500 recognized apostles.

I have the honor of being assigned to preside over this momentous occasion, and I am humbled as I approach the task with an enormous sense of awe.

==
Holy Spirit, I invite Your presence, Your power, and Your direction
==

This is a ceremony celebrating the formal apostolic alignment of Todd Bentley. My first desire is to lay a biblical foundation for what we are about to do.

I will begin with a scripture that has been a central text for those of us who are in the stream of the contemporary apostolic/prophetic movement, **Ephesians 4:11-12:**
And He Himself [Jesus at His ascension] gave some
To be apostles, some prophets, some evangelists
And some pastors and teachers,
For the equipping of the saints for the work of ministry.

The word "equipping" is a translation of the Greek *katartizo* which literally means "aligning," as in setting a broken bone or a chiropractic adjustment. It means putting things in order so that the body functions as it was designed to function. This is one of the responsibilities of apostles such as those whom you see on the platform, and that is the reason we are present tonight. For example, Paul wrote to Titus, "For this reason I left you in Crete, that you should set in order the things that are lacking" (Titus 1:5).

Speaking of Paul and Titus, their relationship is a biblical prototype of apostolic alignment. The same would apply to Paul and Timothy. The apostolic alignment of Timothy and Titus with Paul was a principal factor in

164

allowing God to develop and fulfill His complete destiny in both of their lives.

But Paul himself was also apostolically aligned. Soon after he was called to join Barnabas and his colleagues in Antioch for the then controversial ministry of planting churches among Gentiles, he traveled to Jerusalem to bring a gift for famine relief and also to align with some of the apostles. I want to use the experience that Paul had on that occasion as the text for the protocol for tonight's alignment and commissioning of Todd Bentley. It is found in **Galatians 2:9** which tells the story of one of Paul's visits to Jerusalem:
And when James, Cephas, and John, who seemed to be pillars,
Perceived the grace that had been given to me,
They gave me and Barnabas the right hand of fellowship,
That we should go to the Gentiles and they to the circumcised.

Todd is following Paul's example by inviting to the platform three apostolic pillars of today's church: Ché Ahn of Pasadena, California, Bill Johnson of Redding, California, and John Arnott of Toronto, Canada, Todd's native land. They represent an apostolic network called Revival Alliance.

Notice that the apostles in Jerusalem "perceived the grace that God had given to Paul." "The word "grace" is *charis*, the root of charisma, meaning "spiritual gift or gifts." In Paul's case it was the gift mix necessary to carry the gospel to the Gentiles. In Todd's case it is the gift mix necessary to lead the Lakeland Outpouring.

I have a question for the three apostles: Do you perceive the grace of God given to Todd Bentley as an evangelist to lead the Lakeland Outpouring? [Answer: "I do."]

I have a question for Todd Bentley: Do you recognize the apostolic authority of these three men in your life and ministry, and do you desire to establish an apostolic alignment with them and with Revival Alliance? [Answer: "I do."]

With this affirmation we will move to a formal commissioning, equivalent to "offering the right hand of fellowship" as the three apostles did to Paul in Jerusalem.

This commissioning represents a powerful spiritual transaction taking

place in the invisible world. With this in mind, I take the apostolic authority that God has given me and I decree to Todd Bentley:
- Your power will increase.
- Your authority will increase.
- Your favor will increase.
- Your influence will increase.
- Your revelation will increase.

I also decree that:
- A new supernatural strength will flow through this ministry.
- A new life force will penetrate this move of God.
- A government will be established to set things in their proper order.
- God will pour out a higher level of discernment to distinguish truth from error.
- New relationships will surface to open gates for the future.

===

Che Ahn: It's a miracle that all of these distinguished apostles would all be able to make it all together… with our international commitments, that's a miracle in itself.

Bob Jones prophesied that this Outpouring (and you Todd) would go to a whole different level on June 22 and this is the 23d.

Isaiah 22:22: God is giving the keys of David. He is opening doors that no man can close.

I also think it is significant we have three generations coming together. God is the God of Abraham, Isaac, and Jacob. You know, Todd, we're old enough to be your dad and Peter Wagner is old enough to be your grandfather!

Recognizing that God has chosen you and appointed you to bear much and lasting fruit in this Lakeland revival, and revival around the world; recognizing that He has called you as an Ephesians 4 evangelist and a revivalist, moving in signs and wonders; knowing that you have walked in a manner worthy of the Lord, pleasing Jesus in every way; bearing fruit in every good work; and growing in the intimacy and knowledge of God, we as your brothers and your friends who have a deep love for you, Shonnah, your whole family, just esteem you.

166

We are here to support you. We are here to commission you in the Name of the Father, Son, and the Holy Spirit -- with special oil from Chuck Pierce. It's called "revival oil." Chuck could not make it but he sent this Fed Ex for you (he's in Africa).

So, we anoint you, and commission you in Jesus Name. (Todd falls under the power of God... the three apostles lay hands on him on the floor)

John Arnott: We bless you today, Todd Bentley. You're a friend. You're a man of God. You're a man of prayer. You're a man of the Spirit. You love the anointing. I would say that it's not just the Lakeland Revival, but the whole world goes into revival. And your leading an amazing charge. Multitudes are getting in behind you and saying, "Come on. I'm going to go with you." And so we bless all of that.

Thank you, Holy Spirit, for raising up this young man to lead such a mighty charge around the world, and to partner with God TV and all that has happened here in the last several months now. We bless it in the Name of Jesus. We stand with you and we encourage you, and we honor you.

Bill Johnson: When David wanted Uriah killed, he sent him into battle and then withdrew from him. As a company of people, we refuse to do that. Many revivals throughout history have been cut short of their intention of God's destiny and attention over individuals because of jealousies and fears that get stirred up in the people of God, and we refuse to do that. We shape the course of history by partnering with you, giving honor where it's due.

You welcome the glory as well as anybody I have ever seen in my life. I long to learn from you in that and I bless you. I pray with the rest of these that the measure of the glory would increase. That Moses would no longer be considered the high water mark when the glory shone from his face, but instead, the revelation of the goodness of God would change the face of the church, and that He would use your voice, He would use your grace, your anointing to alter the face of the church before this world. That the goodness of the Lord would be seen once again. I pray this over you in Jesus' Name.

Che Ahn invites the other apostles on the stage to share any words from the Lord for Todd or the Outpouring:

167

Richard Maiden: "For the Lord would say unto thee that this day you have loosed upon this earth what I have wanted for centuries to come forth -- a kingly anointing which will bring in money, money, money. Because the businessmen will rise up and they will go forth under this anointing, and no more will they stay hidden in the shadows. They shall go forth into the political world, into the business world, into the military world and great changes shall take place, saith the Lord, because this night is the night when you started out speaking your first words about the kingdom of God."

Jeff Beacham: "Todd, on behalf of New Zealand, my home country, and Australia, my first adopted country, and America, my third adopted country, I speak favor for you in all those nations. May they receive you supernaturally and may they welcome you and may you be blessed as you go to those nations and blessed as you come back. And let the report be great and mighty from all those nations, in Jesus' Name."

Sharon Stone: "Todd, the Spirit of God says years from now people will look at this time and they will recognize it as when their God showed up and created within the church a new heart, says the Lord. And I will genesis in the midst of the chaos in the world today and I will not just bring a mending, but I will bring forth that which is new, that which is dedicated, that which is decided, that which is pure.

And I will heal the corruptness of the heart, says God, and this is the heart that I will not despise. And as David cried unto me, 'Don't take your Holy Spirit from me,' I have released a cry within my church, says the Lord, that has begun to release its desperation and said, 'I can't live without your presence, I can't live without your glory; I'm undone and I am naked without your presence. No program will be a substitute.' And the Spirit of God says history will measure it by heart."

Paco Garcia: "As Spaniards, we came years ago to this continent and proud to conquer it. Now, we are coming humbly to take this glory to the Spanish-speaking nations of the world. Welcome the revival! Welcome the outpouring to the Spanish-speaking nations of the world!

Welcome to Spain, South America, Latin America, and all over the world." (Paco gives the rest of his word in Spanish here).

168

Bishop Clarice Fluitt: "For the word of the Lord would say, 'Behold a vanguard. Behold the tugboat that is cutting through the ice of religious traditions--the cruel, hard things. The understanding of the mind of man will now bow to the reality of the revelation of the finished work of Calvary. Behold, saith God, you have been equipped with cutting power. You have been equipped to go through those traditions of the mind of man, saith God, and you are pulling the church into the realm of glory. Behind you is a great ship that is laden with healing, deliverance, and prosperity.

This is the word to you, O man of God: Arise, kill and eat. No longer, no longer, no longer will men call unclean what I have called clean.'"

Rick Joyner: "Todd, your ministry is very appropriately named Fresh Fire. And you have certainly been bringing fresh fire. And even when you were going through the dark night of the soul, I thought you had more fire on you than many. The worst state we can ever fall into is lukewarmness and God has sent you as an antidote for that lukewarm spirit.

And the fire has been birthed here; it has been released here. You've unstopped a well. You have other wells to unstop in other cities and other places; this is just the beginning. And there is longevity too. There is increase, but there is also longevity coming. There are many wells, but they are oil wells, and they catch on fire when you unstop them."

Joshua Fowler: "Todd, the Lord has made you to be a detonator. I see cables going around the world to different nations. I see Great Britain being set ablaze by the power of God. I see even as you go into places, God says you'll go with a glory even like William Branham.

And the Lord says you'll carry a portal anointing and whatever city you go over, there will be a portal. There will be a portal that will be opened up, says the Lord. The Lord says you'll detonate and BOOM BOOM BOOM there will be a release of glory to the nations, says the Spirit of the Lord."

Barry Boucher: "Todd, as a fellow Canadian, there is the word HONOR written over you tonight because of Abraham, Isaac and Jacob. You have honored the generations that have gone before you. As a son, you have reached out to the fathers and you have said, 'Bless me.'

And you have blessed us tonight and so we honor you. You've honored the word of God, you've honored the Spirit of God, you've honored the moving the Holy Spirit, and the ways of God. So, tonight, we just affirm that the rest of honor that is upon your life will follow you now in every nation that you go. And you will draw men and women to you that seek honor and want to walk together and want to be what God wants them to be in this generation.

Todd Bentley, the word HONOR rests upon your life."

Stacey Campbell: "Todd, when we were singing that song, *Show Me Your Glory*, I felt impressed to open the scriptures to the very portion of scripture where Moses said, 'Show me Your glory.' And it was the very pinnacle prayer of Moses' life. And this prayer came after a burning bush, came after the release of national judgments, came after going into the cloud of glory and receiving the tablets, and it came after Numbers 24 where Moses went on the mountain with 70 elders and ate and drank with God.

And in this pinnacle prayer, God would not speak face to face with Moses like He did at other times. In this pinnacle prayer of the release of the glory of God, He had to hide Moses in the cleft of the rock. And He had to only show him the hind parts. And He passed by Moses with the unveiling of His glory and He said this: The Lord passed before him and proclaimed, 'The Lord, the Lord God,

(God TV went off the air at this point)
Transcribed by Rhonda Boyer
Edited by Pastor Stephen Strader

Personal note from Pastor Stephen: During the prophetic words and declarations, it was observed by most that a significant RESPONSE took place at the end of Bishop Clarice Fluitt's prophetic word.

I personally believe that TWO very specific and dynamic things took place when she said, "Arise, kill and eat. No longer, no longer, no longer will men call unclean what I have called clean."

First, the phrase is taken from the bible story of Peter's vision on the roof top regarding the sheet filled with unclean animals. This event led to the Jerusalem council which had to make the decision and declaration that the Gospel could now be taken to the Gentiles. To the best of my knowledge, I am not aware of another so PUBLIC strategic council of

170

this kind until June 23, 2008. I believe that this council - this Apostolic Alignment council - made history.

It is my opinion that the RESTORATION of the Five Fold Ministry giftings was COMPLETED by the action of the APOSTLES taking their place in such a PUBLIC display.

Second, the phrase, "No longer, no longer, no longer will men call unclean what I have called clean." I believe that a significant WARNING to the Body of Christ was delivered and that we should all be careful in declaring works of the Holy Spirit to be of the devil.

I also believe that phrase included an antidote for the poison that has already been released, and a declaration to stop any further poison being released into the Body of Christ.

Appendix II

Personal Message from Rory & Wendy
Concerning Lakeland

Beloved GOD TV Viewer,

In the light of many statements having been released about the LAKELAND OUTPOURING and concerning Todd Bentley's marital situation, we sensed that the Lord has released us to write concerning this situation, so that you, our viewers would know our heart concerning this matter.

The first thing we feel led to do is to state unequivocally that in the same manner as the Lord instructed us to broadcast and serve The Call gatherings with Lou Engle; to broadcast what was happening at the International House of Prayer with Mike Bickle; Rick Joyner and Morning Star; the Solemn assembly in San Francisco; Battle Cry and Teen Mania with Ron Luce; Focus on the Family's prayer event for America; the Day of Prayer for the Peace of Jerusalem; and hundreds of other anointed events over the past three years, we believe that the Lord instructed us to broadcast the Outpouring services at Lakeland with Todd Bentley.

It was not a mistake. It was not by mistake. We believe it was a clear instruction from the Lord.

Over the past twelve years, but especially since our launch in America, we have in obedience to the Lord searched through the earth for those events and anointings that the Lord has laid on our hearts – to amplify their message and anointing to the Body of Christ in this crucial end time hour that we live in.

The Lakeland Outpouring with Todd Bentley was one of those events. We received over 45,000 e-mails many, many of these heart rending, powerful testimonies from viewers across the earth of their bodies or their families bodies healed, their lives transformed and their hearts revived. None of us have ever seen such significant fruit in all the years of broadcast.

Far more profound than that were the desperate cries for help. I (Wendy), would go through the live inbox and see the desperate cries from mothers, wives, sons and daughters, so many with TERMINALLY ILL husbands, wives, children, sometimes babies in arms – sensing HOPE in their situation that for so long had been without hope.

Just reading these prayer requests would bring one to tears – We are often so cloistered from the agony of peoples day by day real life agonies - and their agonies were written there. So much so, that we both sensed that would need the word of the Lord under the fear of God to stop these broadcasts with the life changing impact they were having in homes not only in the UK and America but all across the world. And the Glory of the Living God that was being imparted.

We both kept a very close pulse on the revival since the start of its broadcast - we had first hand knowledge of the enormous criticism, persecution and reviling that Todd Bentley was receiving (often we were second contenders for it) but it was Todd Bentley and the Fresh Fire team who received the terrible weight of this.

Todd ministered each day as the revival continued but was consistently and unrelentingly criticized, maligned, persecuted - the attacks grew increasingly violent - and the heartbreaking thing was that so much of it came from the Church.

At the same time, Todd was facing a second wave of attack. This was from the covens, the warlocks - we heard firsthand concerning some of these assignments. The enemy had heard of the great honoring of the Lamb and was determined to destroy it - BY ANY MEANS POSSIBLE AND AT ANY COST.

And the cost was Todd Bentley.

Was it because Todd was vulnerable and certain areas of his life were not surrendered wholly? Yes – like so many of us - in all probability. Was it because the character of Christ was not yet formed in him in the equivalent measure to his gifting? Yes - like so many of us - in all probability.

Could it be the case that there by the grace of God go YOU AND I? Yes - In all probability.

Some of the areas in our lives are watertight and have been honed and refined and polished by the Lord while still other areas in our lives are often still in desperate need of attention. We are an ongoing work and we work out our salvation with fear and trembling.

Well, all ministers who preach should ensure their lives are in order, you may be saying. Yes - we and our board and our minister peers across the globe agree wholeheartedly. And yet, beloved - unfortunately, THERE ARE TIMES when Satan comes unawares and targets a vulnerable area whose weaknesses only become apparent under the most enormous and unrelenting pressure brought to bear.

We believe and of course this is just our personal opinion, that the revival stirred up the satanic realms in a manner that has rarely been seen and with a violent wrath.

It is difficult to understand the degree of spiritual battle that comes against a leader. We have learned we need to protect the move of God with greater prayer for leaders, including ourselves. The body of Christ is growing in greater transparency and accountability, and this too should be a subject of prayer.

Should all of us wait till we are as perfect and as watertight as can be and mature in every area? That, of course, would be the safest course of action, but the truth is that most of us would be 90 years old!

The Lord who made us and knows that we are as dust and yet looks on us with His great mercies and compassions knows this and He the sovereign God of heaven and earth still chooses to take a GOD-risk on you and me every day of our lives. That even under the most intense pressure that we would choose HIM. That we would love HIM. That in times of intense duress and temptation that we would follow HIM.

And let it be so - even more in all our lives, but beloved - let us not forget so many of those who walk in ministry across the earth today with such COURAGE and FERVOR and lay their lives down for HIS CAUSE at great cost to themselves - Todd and Shonnah sowed their lives to sow the seeds of revival and we believe became a supreme target of the enemy.

On the June 23rd, Todd actually spoke openly and with great vulnerability of his and Shonnah's previous marriage challenges and how they had faced those challenges and the Lord had begun His work. He did not try to hide their struggle but shared their ongoing journey.

As Rick Joyner so wisely put it –

"In marriage, I have learned there are those who admit they have been through times when they wondered if their marriage would make it, and then there are liars. Relationships are hard, and the closer they are, the harder they can be. I tell everyone that I give premarital counseling to that the Lord has ordained their marriage in order to kill both of them! That is true. It is also worth it! The greatest gift He gave to man was marriage and family. However, to have a marriage that is good, both will have to die to themselves. If either one does not make the commitment to lay down their life for their mate and their family, then what was meant to be heaven can be hell."

It is an ongoing walk - and we all are ongoing works. But the Lord said something to us some years ago - He said - When you hate sin because it HURTS ME - then it will lose its grip on you. When you hate sin because it displeases ME - its hold diminishes.

The Lord also shared with us that someone can be deceived in an AREA of sin but it does not necessarily mean that in every area of his or her life or ministry, they were walking in deception as some critics of the revival may lean to believe.

And who is to judge that the Lord does not hold the violent unleashing of criticism and faultfinding and tearing down and divisiveness of the heresy hunters, as severe a sin as separation in a marriage? We will find out before the judgment seat in eternity.

One of our greatest grievings has been to see how many in the church backtracked to protect their own reputations. We have been truly refreshed by several close ministry friends with their uncompromising love of truth and lack of a man pleasing spirit that has arisen in the church in the light of the Lakeland aftermath. They have given us fresh courage when we grew weary.

So beloved friend, do we at GOD TV refute the Outpouring? NO.

We are presently planning to broadcast other offshoots of Lakeland in both the United Kingdom and America, including revival meetings in Dudley, England. We have determined in our hearts to follow the Lord with all our might as courageously and as boldly as we can, to reject the pressures to bow to a man pleasing spirit but instead to humble ourselves under the Father's leading. For HE is our all in all. He is our great desire.

Finally, dear friends, while we defend and rejoice in the many ten thousands that God lifted and healed, we also know that there were dear souls, sheep, who were scattered as a result of Todd's personal choices. The Bible says that "hope deferred makes the heart sick" and this is the last thing GOD-TV would want to see happen. We are praying for any that stumbled, and believing that the Lord will restore them to Himself.

Remember: *this was never about Todd Bentley*. It was always about the Holy Spirit and the fact that God loved you and me. It was GOD who touched our lives.

One thing, we felt impressed upon our hearts thirteen years ago when we first launched this ministry. That the Father will allow none of us - whether in ministry or as a viewer to hold idolatry in our hearts for any man. For the Father, The Son and the Holy Spirit alone are to receive our worship.

We continue on the road to maturity. We continue our efforts to serve an end time spiritual army. We continue to try each day to humble ourselves under the mighty hand of the ONLY one who is worthy of ALL adoration. Of ALL HONOUR. Of ALL WORSHIP. Remember also, Jesus Christ is the same yesterday, today and forever. Let's turn our eyes toward Him and away from our trust in man. He who sent His only begotten Son. The Great Father of Compassions. To Him alone we bow.

Personally we believe that the best is yet to come.

For our King and His Kingdom,
Rory and Wendy Alec[38]

Appendix III

History of Christian Outpourings
The Early Church

By
Dr. Karl Strader

The Lakeland Outpouring soon became too large for Ignited, the church where the meetings started. We had to move four times, each to bigger and bigger venues. The morning services, however, continued to be held at Ignited Church. But even those sessions were filled to running over, with 700 to 900 people crowding into the sanctuary and overflow rooms, and the parking lot crammed to overflowing. The night services were then being held in a huge two-football-fields-wide, air-conditioned tent at the airport that can hold up to 10,000 people. It was comfortably filled each night, seven days a week.

To bring such a move of God into perspective with the scriptures, I would like to compare these meetings with the early church and evaluate what's happening. In the church formed after the Resurrection and the coming of the Holy Spirit to birth the Body of Christ, the following things took place:

GREAT POWER (Acts 4:33)
The power of God was evident in the first church, with the Holy Spirit in leadership. Signs and wonders were done by the Apostles, as well as the other believers, to confirm the Word. The Gospel was demonstrated. It attracted the attention of the entire community.

GREAT GRACE (Acts 4:33)
The favor of God was evident. God's grace brought about a beautiful prosperity to what was going on that was more than notable. The townspeople were amazed at what was transpiring in their midst. Many

new converts were made. There was a unity of believers that was almost unbelievable as they ministered to one another and unto the Lord in the temple and from house to house.

GREAT FEAR (Acts 5:5, 11)

As Ananias and Sapphira were dramatically corrected, a holy fear came upon all the church. This wasn't hype, this was revival. It was God working through His people. Everyone knew that it was God and not man who was displaying His mighty power. People were awestruck, amazed at what was happening.

GREAT COMPANY (Acts 6:7)

Do you remember how Christ on the cross prayed for those "who know not what they do?" His prayer was answered as many priests repented of their terrible sin of being instrumental in nailing Him to the cross, and believed as they saw the miraculous and the supernatural unfold before their eyes. When the religious leaders repent openly, we know we are in revival!

GREAT AFFLICTION (Acts 7:11, 11:28)

The devil was stirred up. No way can we have a move of God without the devil attempting to do a number on us. He's angry. He hates everything that glorifies God. He will begin to stir up controversy, sickness, and natural disasters, to try the faith and the patience of the saints.

GREAT PERSECUTION (Acts 8:1)

Whenever God moves we can expect that not everyone is happy with revival. "Religious" people are not happy once they see their lifestyle and their control over the community jeopardized. There is no way, if we start doing the will of God "in earth as it is in heaven" that we won't have persecution from the devil's crowd. They hate God, and they hate us!

GREAT LAMENTATION (Acts 8:2)

Tragedies take place in the midst of revival. It brings great sorrow to the church. There should be no sadness in our ranks, ever. But sorrow, yes. Part of being a Christian is to have great compassion for our fellow believers. Tears will come to our eyes when difficult times come, but God will be right there to comfort us and put His arms around us.

GREAT JOY (Acts 8:8, 15:3)

"Outpourings" or "visitations" always bring laughter and rejoicing. God is a great God. His presence overwhelms our emotions. It's not "funny" or necessarily humorous, but it's the excitement and joy of the Lord that manifests itself. In fact, we will be "drunk" with the mighty manifestation of God's "closeness" to us.

GREAT SUFFERING (Acts 9:16)

Suffering is a definite part of being God's child. Many do not warn people enough about the "hardness" of being in the family of God. His yoke is "easy" and His burden is "light", but we infuriate Satan when we "sell out" to God. He and all of the demons of hell will attack us at every turn of the road. It's impossible to avoid pain as a believer if we truly are "Godly." It's a part of the turf!

GREAT NUMBERS (Acts 11:21, 14:1)

Not just the priests, but believers will be added, daily, and over the long haul, multitudes will be included. Some say that numbers are not important, but in God's church, if we follow the pattern of the first church after the resurrection and after the Holy Spirit came, not only will believers be added, but the masses will become hungry and thirsty for righteousness. We can expect that to be an integral part of the Kingdom of God.

Great Awakenings

We need to pray for Great Awakenings of the people, not only in our nation, but throughout the nations of the world. Even though this old world will continue to "wax worse and worse" until the visible coming of our Lord, there's still plenty of room for revival, "outpourings", and awakenings. Even then, by comparison to the billions now living, there will still only be "a few" that will finally make it into heaven!

Since the time of the original Apostles, after Jesus went back to be with His Father in heaven, there have been a number of outpourings of the Holy Spirit with revival fires burning, souls being saved, and signs and wonders confirming the Word. We have very little, as far as records are concerned, for the first millennium. History began to record unusual phenomena that began to take place in the years just before Columbus discovered America.

Savonarola

Born in 1452, Savonarola was a monk in the Roman Church in Italy. Quiet, retiring, serious, and subdued, he spent many hours fasting and praying. The lonely places, the open fields, were his meditation habitat. He spent much time weeping and singing songs to the Lord. He was grieved over the people of the world which he felt were like the folks in Sodom and Gomorrah.

The Bible was Savonarola's textbook. He thundered from the Catholic Church's pulpits a thousand woes that he saw would befall the people if they didn't repent. The thousands that heard him responded by bringing their witchcraft and pornographic items, piled them in the town square 60 feet high and 240 feet in circumference, and publicly burned them.

Florence was transformed. Street urchins and hoodlums, who had been singing ribald songs before, began to sing hymns in the public places. Savonarola's success in reaching out to people was short-lived, however. The officials of the city and the church had him arrested and he was burned at the stake!

George Fox

In the 17th century, George Fox was born in England. The churches were dead and formal in his time. Independent from the Anglican Church, he felt it was necessary to discard the ordinances of the church, like water baptism and communion, because, in his thinking, they were so formal that they had *lost their meaning*.

George Fox started the Quaker movement in the late 1600's. Sleeping in the haystacks in the fields, he led a very primitive life, wearing a suit made from leather. He opposed slavery, emphasized spiritual worship, opposed warfare, fought imprisoning debtors, but encouraged honesty in business ventures. He—and other Quakers—were persecuted, stoned, beaten and imprisoned, perhaps more than any other living men. At one time, there were more than 4,500 Quakers imprisoned in England and Wales.

One time Fox remained in a trance for 14 days. After that experience people began to shake when he spoke. He had England, Scotland, and Wales ablaze with revival. His eyes flashed and his voice was like thunder to the thousands that heard him speak. His message to the people was that men should be meek in spirit, pure in heart, and have a great love for God and neighbor.

John Wesley

John Wesley, born in 1703, shook the British Isles and America. He probably could be counted as one of the deepest spiritual leaders since the Apostles.

When John Wesley spoke to thousands of people in the open air, (sometimes numbering as many as 20,000), of course, without a public address system, the people trembled and shook because of conviction of sin. He taught instantaneous conversion.

One night, when a group of about 60 ministers met for prayer, with Wesley leading, the power of God descended upon them, and they fell to the floor, at 3:00 in the morning. The power of the Spirit brought a manifestation of great joy into their midst.

Although Wesley, as an Oxford graduate, avoided fleshly excitements, hallucinations, and delusions, he was careful not to quench the Spirit. People cried out to God, frequently falling to the ground as dead, and others trembled violently, with heavy groaning and crying. Opposing Quakers and Episcopalians often mobbed him, but many of them fell down in violent agony before they could do him harm.

For much of his life, Wesley rode his horse as a means of transportation around 8,000 miles a year. As a habit, he would rise at 4:00 a.m. and be preaching by 5:00 o'clock!

These periods of history were described as fruitful outpourings of the Spirit of God. God has His time to give certain ministers in His Kingdom a great harvest of souls in sovereign moves of His Spirit. But whether it is an unusual outpouring or an "in between" time, there's always been the opportunity for people to respond to the drawing power of the Holy Spirit to Jesus so that they could receive salvation and the promise of Eternal Life!

Early Outpourings in America

Long after John Wesley's day, a remarkable "outpouring" occurred at Cane Ridge, Kentucky, at the turn of the 19th century. In 1801, a Pentecostal-like meeting took place in the center of the eastern half of the United States. It was the beginning of the camp meetings that were to be found all across our country until this day. This meeting had a great effect on our whole nation.

Unusual phenomena took place in the Cane Ridge meetings. Even though Presbyterian ministers were initially involved, Methodist ministers were in leadership, also. However, the unusual manifestations were more Pentecostal than anything else. Soon "the floor of the Red River Presbyterian church was 'covered with the slain' while their screams pierced the heavens. Vinson Synan, in his book, *The Holiness-Pentecostal Tradition*, described that era of worship.

Accustomed to 'braining bears and battling Indians', they received their religion with great color and excitement. Their 'Godly hysteria' included such manifestations as falling, jerking, barking like dogs, falling into trances, the 'holy laugh' and such wild dances as David performed before the Ark of the Lord.

In August 1801 the Cane Ridge revival reached a climax when crowds variously estimated from 10,000 to 25,000 gathered. In the light of blazing campfires hundreds of sinners would fall 'like dead men in a mighty battle.' Others would get the 'jerks' and shake helplessly in every joint. Peter Cartwright reported that in one service he saw five hundred jerking at once. The unconverted were as subject to the 'jerks' as were the saints. One minister reported that 'the wicked are much more afraid of it than of small pox or yellow fever.'

After 'praying through' some would crawl on all fours and bark like dogs, thus 'treeing the devil.' Others would fall into trances for hours, awakening to claim salvation or sanctification. In some services entire congregations would be seized by the 'holy laugh,' an ecstasy that could hardly be controlled.

The most amazing phenomenon was the 'singing exercise' whereby the saints 'in a very happy state of mind would sing most melodiously, not from the mouth or nose, but entirely in the breast.'

They swooned away and lay for hours in the straw prepared for those 'smitten of the Lord', or they started suddenly to flee away and fell prostrate as if shot down by a sniper, or they took suddenly to jerking with apparently every muscle in their body until it seemed they would be torn to pieces or converted into marble, or they shouted and talked in unknown tongues.[39]

So it was in the Cane Ridge revival in Kentucky at the beginning of the 1800's.

If God doesn't change, and if Jesus is the same, yesterday, and today and forever, then why would we *not* think that as people acted when the Holy Ghost came on the Day of Pentecost, that would not happen again if the season were ripe for it? The Bible prophesies that in the last days, before the coming of Christ, the Spirit will be outpoured upon all flesh. From the beginning of this last century, starting in 1901 until the present day, well over 500 million people have received the Pentecostal experience around the world. Is the time short before the Coming of the Lord, or what?!

Great Awakenings in America

There have been four Great Awakenings in America.

The First Great Awakening came during the years of the Colonies, 1730's and the 1740's, with the Congregationalists and the Presbyterians in New England. Jonathan Edwards and George Whitfield are names to remember as great, thundering leaders. Dramatic, emotional manifestations accompanied the preaching of the Word.

The Second Great Awakening took place in the time between the 1790's through the 1840's. Emphasis was on prison reform, temperance, women's suffrage, and abolition of slavery. Charles Finny and Peter Cartwright were names prominent during this season.

The Third Great Awakening happened during the 1850's through the early 1900's, bringing with it the Social Gospel, the Holiness Movement, Dwight L. Moody's crusades, the forming of the YMCA, the Epworth League, and the coming of the Salvation Army to America. Starting in

---

39   Synan, Vinson, *The Holiness-Pentecostal Tradition: Charismatic Movements in the Twentieth Century,* William B. Eerdman's Publishing, 1997.

1906, the Azusa Street Pentecostals were birthed.

The Fourth Great Awakening took place during the 1960's and 1970's, with the mushrooming of the Southern Baptists, the Missouri Synod, and the rise of the Fundamentalists, the Jesus People, and the Charismatics.

Advent of Signs and Wonders

The immediate background for the Lakeland Outpouring was the advent of the end-time signs and wonders of people like William Branham, A.A. Allen, and Jack Coe, along with familiar names like Kenneth Hagin, Oral Roberts, Kathryn Kuhlman, Benny Hinn, and Reinhart Bonke.

William Branham: Born in Kentucky in 1909 to an alcoholic father, William Branham had a Roman Catholic background. His home was impoverished. He had many visions; one in particular, a man appeared to him admonishing him to abstain from drinking, smoking and illicit sex so that he could carry the healing revival to the nations. Promoted by Gordon Lindsay and the *Voice of Healing*, he preached to great crowds such as in Durbin, South Africa to 45,000 people. He, through the Word of Knowledge, could read many people's "mail," with people around him saying, "He never missed." He was surrounded by controversy.

A.A. Allen: A. A. Allen, 1911-1970, also had an alcoholic father. He had a Methodist background. His mother was a Cherokee Indian. His home was in Arkansas. Influenced by Oral Roberts, Allen purchased a tent seating 10,000, and later bought another that would hold 22,000. Someone gave him a track of land of 1280 acres, where he had his headquarters and built a Bible School. He was on radio and cast out devils on television, as well as preached and healed the sick. He, too, was surrounded by controversy.

Jack Coe: Jack Coe, 1918-1956, had an alcoholic father and was born into deep privation in Oklahoma City. He attended Southwestern Bible Institute in Enid, Oklahoma, joined the army, and then was credentialed, for a short time, with the Assemblies of God. He was co-editor of the *Voice of Healing* magazine with Gordon Lindsay, and purchased a tent, seating 22,000. He was arrested in Miami for "practicing medicine without a license," but was acquitted after so many validated testimonies of divine healing came to the attention of the courts. His son, Jack Coe,

Jr. is in the healing ministry today.

The Fifth Great Awakening, Perhaps?

It is possible that since this meeting in Lakeland has become a "media" revival, with God-TV spreading the news through 214 nations and the internet going to every nation in the world, this could start the Fifth Great Awakening, not only for America, but the entire planet. It is spreading throughout the nations, including China and India, and especially throughout Europe, from where many people flew in to witness the phenomenon.

RECOMMENDED READING:

ACCESS GRANTED and ID REQUIRED
Dr. Joshua Fowler

 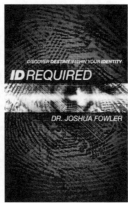

For more annointed books:
www.LMGpublishing.com

Legacy Media Group
"Publishing for Generations"

For additional resources of Stephen Strader:
www.ignitedchurch.com

For booking information:
www.stephenstrader.org

To contact Stephen Strader:
stephenstrader@gmail.com

RECOMMENDED MUSIC:

www.kelihornmusic.com
http://www.myspace.com/kelihornmusic

Scott Van Wagner "I Expect Wonders"
www.ignitedchurch.com

Photography by:

Ryan Charles Harmening
Ryan Charles Photography
www.ryancharlesphotography.com